To those who strive, dare to dream and believe in life-long learning.

For all family and friends who starred in this epic journey.

Paul Franklin

WHITE SOCKS
AND CHALK DUST

An outrageously amusing and poignant true story

AUSTIN MACAULEY PUBLISHERS™

LONDON • CAMBRIDGE • NEW YORK • SHARJAH

A CIP catalogue record for this title is available from the British Library.

ISBN 9781398461833 (Paperback)
ISBN 9781398461840 (ePub e-book)

www.austinmacauley.com

First Published 2022
Austin Macauley Publishers Ltd
1 Canada Square
Canary Wharf
London E14 5AA

DISCLAIMER:

Some of the names of individuals featured in this book have been changed to protect identities. Some haven't, so live with it!

Chapter One

THE CHALLENGE

"OI, PASS the tomato sauce, you lanky streak of piss!"

The outburst from our rather diminutive, inebriated bass player, was wrong on two levels; firstly, we were dining in a public place and secondly, Piet had ordered a traditional moussaka which didn't require it!

Piet always got drunk easily; both on and off stage, but he was, by some country mile, the best musician in our humble group 'The Bridgemen'. The name derived from the town where we all grew up, chronologically speaking – Bridgeford. He could adapt to any style of music and he enjoyed immersing himself in the ambience of any gig. I always felt that he looked like Kermit the frog playing the bass to Rick our front man's Miss Piggy.

Bert, our harmonica player, would often imitate Fozzie Bear drinking a pint; exaggerating the opening of his mouth and consuming half his drink in one gulp!

He used to complain about being dizzy through playing too many 'suck notes'. He was always ribbing me about how I was at an advantage in the looks department...not hard in his case! His attractiveness to the fairer sex came not necessarily from physical attributes, but rather quirky, archaic, endearing comedic qualities; not to mention his eccentricity. Like all of us, he could reveal some annoy-ing habits, such as picking his ears and upon inspecting the content, eating it! I recall children doing this at school and after some lengthy consideration could only conclude it was because they were disgusting individuals!

At times He would try and embarrass me on stage, as on one occasion when out of the blue he pipes up into the microphone with:

"The way you talk about sex anyone would think you'd had it!"

Unconsciously, this time, I replied:

"The way you talk about sex anyone would *know* you'd never had it!

That prompted a ripple of laughter from the audience and indeed from Bert too. Mine was an impulsive response, but it left me with a feeling of one-upmanship.

I suppose Derek, our banjo player, was more akin to the muppets' gofer Scooter, but was a remarkable player in the Earl Scruggs style. He doubled up on the guitar and did some singing/song-writing, but he begrudgingly acknowledged my vocal strengths.

Bert always called him 'Light and Hippie' because he always ordered a light and bitter combination; a popular beverage of the '60s and '70s, mainly because people thought they were getting more drink for their money.

We all of us used to regard Niall's less-than-average fiddle skills as a 'bridge too far'. I remember the time only too well, when, as on so many occasions we were invited to play at the local mental health hospital at Shenley. The Shenley Hospital gig was always a source of much surprise and interruptions were always on the menu.

We had always engaged in a diverse range of gigs from concerts to barn dances, even weddings and funerals. This was possible because of the differences in skillsets within the group. I think it's fair to say that Rick wasn't the most melodious of singers, but he had a wide-ranging repertoire of songs and quotes that could allow him to perform in front of a multitude of audiences at differently themed events.

In fact, I nicknamed him 'Click-in Cassette-head' because he had a library of music for almost any genre: Folk, Irish, American Bluegrass, Country and Western, Popular, Blues and Rock and Roll.

He would often start a set by requesting the audience not to take photographs for security reasons...social security reasons. His finishing line was inevitably:

"If you have enjoyed yourselves half as much as we have, then we must have enjoyed ourselves twice as much as you."

He was a big hit with the residents of Shenley, especially for these reasons.

It all began quite innocuously with a patient asking Niall if he could play his fiddle. Niall refused over the microphone, but this individual was insistent...so was Niall!

After the first set, the band took a quick break. Niall had gone to get a cup of tea and now this was the patient's chance. He strode up to the stage and picked up the violin. No one else in the band stopped him. There was always the chance he'd break it! However, this elderly man quite adeptly retuned the instrument and then began playing a concerto with much expression and musical accomplishment, to all our astonishment. His musicality, interpretation and level of ability were truly entertaining!

Now, at some point, Derek, seizing a perfect opportunity, asked the chap if he knew any of the pieces to our second set. He replied:

"Tell me the key, you play, and I'll follow."

Well, we did and started playing before Niall could get back. All I can say is that we sounded a lot more professional than when we turned up! This man was amazing and obviously had a classical background. Niall understandably (to flirt recklessly with the understatement) was embittered and of course tried to regain ownership of his violin. We, the rest of the band, wouldn't let him, so he angrily performed a symbolic military turn and went, leaving his instrument behind. We never saw him again. The programme was a great hit with staff, patients and band members alike!

We offered his instrument to the patient who politely refused, saying that he had a better one. We later tried to get a release for him to play other gigs with us, but administrative bureaucracy wouldn't allow it. We all felt dejected about this and realised that if he had performed on our LP recording at Abbey Road, we should have appeared on *Top of the Pops* by now!

Occasionally, we heard news from Rick about Niall's later ventures and were interested to know that he had set up a dog kennel business; not that interested, mind, until we learned that he had taken in an Alsatian and Shih Tzu the same week and the former had eaten the latter!

Rick said that it had taken some explaining to the owners when they returned from holiday. The whole event prompted a recollection of that callous, although wholly appropriate, phrase 'dog eat dog'.

However unfortunate Niall's departure and unsuccessful ventures were, worse was to come. When I saw him at a reunion concert many years later, he was sporting a beard and glasses which made him look *exactly* like Rolf Harris!

Meanwhile, back at the Greek restaurant, Piet had fallen face first into the leftovers of his dish with a glowing cigarette between his fingers. We had all become a little worse for wear, but I was feeling a little more confident engaging Rick in a debate. I rather foolishly challenged him to a discussion involving politics. Yes, I should have known better! Rick had gone up against Cecil

Parkinson in the Hertsmere elections as the Labour candidate.

Although maudlin at times, Rick was a big gun in this department. He was 'an intellect', highly intelligent and very well read. In fact, what we teachers would regard as a reader as opposed to someone who could read. He would consume books as if they were food. He could eat his way from here to China... and China's a bloody long way!

Well suffice to say, I didn't last long... went down like a flamer with Rick's cannon-shell words resonating in my ears!

"What do you know about politics? you're just a *Sun* reader! He said.

I wasn't, but I might just as well have been.

To add further injury by way of his rapier wit he continued with his character assassination:

"What you know about politics you could write on the back of a postage stamp in aircraft sky-writing with enough room left over for the Lord's prayer in a bold flowing hand!"

Both Rick and Fozzy were teachers. Rick had gone through the lengthier process of a degree, whilst Bert, who had been in primary teaching for much longer, had a teaching certificate. Bert could have progressed much further in teaching if he hadn't been trapped in the 19th century using archaic terminology, loquacious vaunting and imagining himself to be Dickens' Mr Gradgrind.

Conversely, Rick couldn't have progressed in teaching because he was far too emotional and too much of a politician. Indeed, he ended up as a teaching union representative...and a good one at that.

Nevertheless, having lost round one emphatically, I challenged both Rick and Bert in their educational capacities, announcing confidently, though less modestly, that

11

I could easily do their jobs and even progress further than they. Rick and Bert pounced on the declaration like bloodhounds and upped the ante by giving me a time limit including that necessary to secure me a degree.

At the end of the evening, I left the restaurant feeling more sober and rather more trepidatious about my prospects. After all, I was a Corona soft drinks mobile retailer with a franchise and was to further education what sumo wrestlers were to the pole vault.

Moreover, my future was founded on a bet! How was I to know that I was going to embark upon the biggest challenge of my life, which would eventually see me reaching the top of my profession and not with a few incidences along the way?

Just like the flightless 'Big Bird', this 'Muppet' was going to find the route to success, a tough mountain to climb.

Chapter Two

THE LONG TREK

I COULDN'T pursue a teaching degree at Wall Hall Teacher-Training College without an O-level in maths and an A-level of some kind, having failed them epically at school, but at least they had given me a conditional offer. However, I knew this was going to be a long haul over two years because I couldn't work and study at the same time – knowing my limitations only too well! I applied to follow a course in Business Maths in St Albans College in 1987 and, with a lot of application over the year, came out with a 'B' grade.

This indeed gave me the momentum to enrol for the A-level language and literacy course, which I found exacting though liberating.

To be fair, Rick was helping me in the background proof-reading my essays and allowing me to do voluntary teaching at his school in Milton Keynes.

He invited me up to his flat on one occasion and upon opening the door, I was horrified to lay eyes on the interior.

"Welcome to 'Squalor Mansions'!" he exclaimed.

The main room was in a terrible state: extremely dirty and unpleasant, or so I thought until I saw the kitchen, which needed a risk assessment before entering! Rick, like some other intellects I know, was oblivious to the surroundings of his accommodation. Indeed, the very act of cleaning was anathema to him. Having been brought up as an only child, his mother had spoilt and precluded him from engaging in such trivial matters as hygiene. Honestly, I'd seen cleaner watering holes on Attenborough documentaries. Nevertheless, I spent some time helping him to regain some equilibrium of living standards, before going out for a meal and planning the next day in Rick's school.

I remember, on one occasion, when I was giving a musical set to his class, that Rick was very disgruntled by the inattention of one boy in Year Five. To my astonishment, Rick appeared to launch himself across the seated audience and grab this individual, terrifying him and frightening the rest of the class and myself to boot. By today's standards, and even then I suspect, this was tantamount to assault and clearly the result of someone nearing the loss of ability to function. True enough, Rick left teaching soon after this event. I suppose this unfortunate occurrence presented itself as some kind of premonition to the future demands of teaching. However, a bet was a bet!

I successfully completed my A-level studies and again achieved a 'B' grade. My tutor was disappointed. She had expected an 'A' and we both knew where it had gone wrong! One of the exam questions was... 'Compare and Contrast the Metaphysical Works of Donne and Marvell'. I couldn't do this at the time because I had literally memorized the works and interpretative notes of both poets and it was all I could do but regurgitate this information separately.

These results would have greatly pleased my chemistry tutor at school, who gleefully though unsympathetically said she would wear a cabbage on her head as a hat if I passed my exams. There was no risk of that happening!

Ironically, the hobbies and pastimes which had distracted me from achieving my grades, first and second times around, such as music, acting and sport, were eventually to become valuable assets in my future teaching career.

I was beginning to appreciate the limitations of my intellectual capabilities. Nevertheless, I had now gained the required entry qualifications to my teaching degree course. During this two-year period leading up to my acceptance, I would earn monies playing in the Bridgemen and often frequented the folk music evenings at the Red Lion pub in Bridgeford, where Paul Simon, no less, once played in his earlier career. The building has now been taken over by McDonald's, but at the time the pub was a dive and a magnet for the endless wave and surge of lowlifes in the vicinity. Heckling and fights were frequent.

I remember vividly one evening, when Piet's younger brother Saul was performing a set as a soloist on the guitar. He was a cadaverous-looking individual with the singing talents of one, but he was by no means the oddest of the gathering. Nonetheless, when he offered the audience the chance to ask for requests, one indomitable, and some might say prescient, individual said: "Yes, give up and fuck off!"

Bert turned up late (though not as late as my brother and father, who I relied upon for moral and protective support) and Saul rather stupidly said to him: "Sit down, you're late!"

To which Bert replied: "If I had known you were playing, I wouldn't have turned up at all!"

That did it! Saul indignantly threw down his guitar and stormed off. I was up next.

In retrospect, I shouldn't have bothered. The evening was shrouded in misgivings.

I took to the stage and started an introduction to a John

Denver song, at which point a mocking and contemptible individual blurted out:

"We know what songbook you got for Christmas."

"The last time I saw a mouth like that, Lester Piggott was riding behind it!" I replied.

I carried on playing the introduction with my twelve-string. My six-string Fender was on a stand near the toilet door.

As I progressed well into the lyrics of the song and matters had seemingly settled down, suddenly and swiftly out of the toilet came an unwelcome distraction. An undesirable character snatched my Fender from its stand and ran across the room to the exit. In that instance, a chap of medium build, whom I had never seen before got up and gave chase. I quickly followed. No one else I knew did. However, some finger-stuck-in-the-ear folk singer called Bob did get up and adopt a preposterous pose, like a forgotten age comic-caricature, and shouted: "Stop thief!" Like he would have…

"Oh! You mean me? Sorry, it's a fair cop. I thought I was going to get away with that."

Meanwhile, I was running after this criminal who fled down the street. I couldn't see the unknown character who had followed him out ahead of me, but that didn't occupy my mind for very long as my quarry, seeing me gain on him, let go of my stolen guitar which clattered upon the ground. Pumped up and seething with anger, I followed him across a main road and was slightly confused to hear a taxi driver shout from his window:

"Oi! How many of you does it take to beat up a bloke on his own?"

That was irrelevant as I caught my prey. And, as I was giving him a lesson in etiquette, I was suddenly spun around and faced with no less than six individuals, who set about me.

I was brutally head-butted and although I couldn't see through my blood-spattered face, I kept punching the guy I had hold of. That was until I was forced to the ground whereupon, I sustained a number of kicks to the head.

The last image I saw before passing out, was this group of assailants dragging off my guitar thief, obviously worse for wear. When I came round, Fozzy's face was bearing down on me. *"This couldn't be Heaven,"* I thought.

"Hello, my mate, we wondered where you'd got to. Someone's rung your family. That other bloke's in a bad way."

He of course meant the Good Samaritan who had quickly responded to the situation. As Bert spoke, it quickly became apparent to me what events had taken place. The thief had had accomplices waiting outside the building, ready to apprehend anyone brave enough to chase him. This of course accounted for the quick demise of my unknown friend and the subsequent chase of the pack after me! The taxi driver had naturally presumed that seven individuals were chasing this single guy.

Peter, my brother, was quickly on the scene, having brought my father with him on his powerful motorbike.

"Sorry, bro, should have been here," he rather guiltily announced.

To be fair, if they had been, that group of thugs wouldn't have stood a chance. The pair of them were both built like proverbial shithouses and when we were together, no one would dare to bother us. Indeed, I remember the time my sisters had gained the unwanted attentions of a stranger. When we turned up on the scene, this fellow said to us that he was only asking for the time. Peter replied:

"I can help you there, mate…it's drip-feed time."

My father is a kind and generous man but, back in the

day, when wronged, he defined the word 'intimidating'. I'd need to write another book about his capers.

They took me to the local hospital. I spent most of the night there with concussion and a broken nose. Three operations later, I'm still, all these years later, suffering from chronic rhinitis, with smell, taste and breathing difficulties.

After this rather unfortunate event, it's perhaps true to say that I became a little intolerant of my band colleagues and, combined with growing pressures at teacher training, I left the group.

In pursuit of my B.Ed (Hons), I studied Historical Geography as the main degree subject, with Music the basis of the 'Honours' award.

My wife, who often ridicules my navigational and directional skills on car journeys, suggests that I must have studied 'Hysterical Geography'.

My history tutor (whose name shamefully escapes me) made a lasting impact on me with his introductory talk. He always insisted that children learn best through their bodies. If you teach them about the first powered flight, give them a stopwatch and get them to run one-hundred yards in exactly twelve seconds. If they want to know how heavy Colt 45 guns were, fill socks with sand and strap them to their waists.

He commenced his pitch with a quote: "When the best leaders' work is done...others will say we did it ourselves." (Lao Tzu, 6th century B.C.) This quote helped to secure me my last Headship post.

I found the demands of the course very difficult and admit, at times, considered ditching the whole idea. Nevertheless, I made a resolution... if I successfully completed the first year, I'd continue to the bitter end; thus extending my further education and learning renaissance by six years!

Rick guided me through my 'Child Study' assignment which featured Toni, the daughter of Leslie and Danny; both of whom I met in the Middle East. (See below.)

I remember observing the five-year-old with two dolls, one black and one white. She was combing the hair of the white doll and this prompted me, with racial equality in mind, to comment on why she wasn't combing the hair of the black doll. She replied:

"Cos I can't get this comb through her hair, silly. I need to use this comb for my black baby."

Upon which she picked up an Afro comb and thrust it under my nose.

I adore the refreshing ingenuousness of young children who in the most loving and unbiased environments are naturally 'colour-blind' and the best ambassadors for racial harmony.

There were no tutoring fees to be repaid upon the completion of courses back in the day and I was very happy to receive a ninety per cent grant towards my fees and living expenses.

I found some occasional work, such as bricklaying and dry-stone walling, to help make ends meet, as I'd had to sell (well, half-sell; I didn't get all the money) the franchise because of time constraints.

At the end of one such project, the employer asked if I would like to accept an old left-hand drive Datsun Cherry in part-payment. Having no means of transport to call my own, I duly accepted. I drove this vehicle for over four years and was amazed at how it kept going, even when parts failed and even fell off!

Whilst on teaching practice, the starter-motor packed in, so I used to park it on a hill and bump-start it, going to and from work.

A year after I finished my degree, I received a letter from the college asking me to remove the car I'd dumped (well forgotten about) in their car park. This I did and *drove* the car to a scrap dealer who gave me a tenner for it. It actually sparked into life after remaining unused for over a year!

I'd have no compunction about buying Japanese technology today. It's served me well!

As a 'fresher' I had accommodation on site and the opportunity over the months, to make some good friends. One of these was Paul, an undergraduate electrical engineer. We forged a great alliance and had much fun, until tragedy struck.

Like me, Paul was older than most freshers. He was dating and co-habiting with a beautiful young first-year student. One evening he was repairing a desk lamp belonging to her. He pulled out the plug (or so he thought) to the light, which he began to strip down to the pins which connect the light bulb to the voltage. Four *identical* plugs had been inserted into an extension lead and Paul had mistakenly extracted the wrong one, leaving the lamp live. He grabbed the pins and let out a cry of help to his girlfriend before the amperage subdued him.

Pausing for a moment's thought, or even a modicum of common sense would have told her to simply flip the main switch; even more dramatically, to strike his grasp with a non-conductive implement, or even shoulder-barge him off the connection.

She chose instead to run for help. By the time we arrived on the scene, he was dead!

The irony of his unfortunate and dreadful demise was all too apparent and might have been the subject of amusement if he had merely received an unexpected, non-fatal shock.

The resulting post-mortem and insensitive accusations were the cause of her abandoning the course.

Inevitably, other students left the college in the first year; mainly through the demands of their courses.

I recall having a conversation with an engineering student over an evening meal in the dining hall. He was displeased with his choice of degree and began ranting on about how the teaching course was so much easier. He erroneously believed we all 'knocked-off' at three-thirty and enjoyed fifteen weeks of holiday. He wasn't the first numbskull to come to this conclusion. I'd had this inane conversation with others before. This time, worn down by the fatuous comments, I actively supported his theory and suggested he got an immediate transfer to the teaching course, as it was an easy option. Life couldn't get any easier, I declared and it didn't take the idiot long to be persuaded.

I met up with him before the end of the term, just before his decision to leave. His parting comment to me was: "You complete bastard."

I told him he wasn't the first and *definitely* not the last to make the mistake of thinking teachers had an easy option.

Chapter Three

REACHING BASE CAMP

OCCASIONAL WORK was all very well and good, but when the long holiday breaks came, I needed some regular income. Then an old brass-band friend of mine suggested that I do some part-time VIP chauffeuring with his London-based firm. I confessed that I'd never driven in that capacity before, but he insisted that if I planned my routes well and dressed well in a suit, I'd pull it off. Richard put in a good word for me and drove me to London for an interview. When I was asked if I knew London well, I lied and said yes. Somehow, I got the job.

The following day I had to drive to Heathrow in a stretch Mercedes limousine to pick up three separate individuals who needed to be brought back to their respective hotels in central London.

I asked my controller for the details of the addresses, but she couldn't confirm them. I was to ask the passengers upon arrival at the airport. This prospect filled me with dread as I'd be driving blind. Nevertheless, I set off.

I eventually, and I think quite professionally, got all the passengers to the freshly cleaned car and loaded their luggage and persons within. One of them was disabled and stowing her wheelchair was tricky, but possible. The boot space was generous.

So, off we went, amidst general happy chatter, eventually finding myself driving up the Cromwell Road. Then the wheels fell off, figuratively speaking. In trying to find all three hotels, I stopped and asked no fewer than seven pedestrians along the way. They were all foreign and had little or no idea. Then, as luck would have it, I spotted, stopped and asked a policeman, who equally had no idea.

My endearing and lasting reminiscence of this mini catastrophe was catching sight of the redoubtable, disabled lady peering into an *A-to-Z* of London I'd left on the back seat, to help me complete my foiled mission.

I finally resorted to a preplanned emergency coded message on an oversized brick of a mobile phone. "POB en route to..." My controller was wonderful, if too late under the circumstances. She advised me of certain roadblocks on the way to the hotels I'd named, in order to redirect me back on course. At the cost of one pound a minute, she got the weary travellers to their destinations, within thirty minutes.

The disabled lady was the last to be dropped and as I was nearing her hotel, I drove across Westminster Square. She exclaimed in her Canadian accent, upon sighting the Palace of Westminster: "What's that beautiful building?"

To which I replied: "I don't know, it wasn't there yesterday."

She immediately erupted into laughter and stated that my amusing comment had just earned me a tip!

She was a lovely, understanding lady; all the more remarkable for the fact that she shared the colossal fee of £300 with her fellow passengers, having endured a less than average, unprofessional taxi journey.

The only VIP aspect of their trip was the beautiful car... driven by a cerebral bankrupt!

On the second day...yes there was one, surprisingly, I was assigned to a Mrs Arab, although that wasn't her real name, I suspect.

She wanted to go to a hairdresser in central London. I resourcefully memorized the route and set off to pick her up.

Upon arrival at the hairdresser, she asked me to wait and then take her to another residence. I asked if she would tell me the address, but it was almost as if she suspected I should be undone and exposed for the fraud I was and replied that she'd tell me when she got back.

As she got back in, I commented on her hair…why!!!??? She graciously, if with somewhat unease, accepted the comment of admiration and informed me of the destination.

I stumbled and rather uncomfortably asked her for the general direction. She paused momentarily and then gave a wry smile:

"You're new to this, aren't you? How long have you been chauffeuring?"

I felt a little relief at having been found out:

"Just two days."

She smiled warmly and said she'd get me there:

"Just set off in the direction of the Edgware Road."

I did and at the next corner drove up a one-way street, the wrong way! She rather calmly told me that I'd gone up a one-way street:

"Yes," I replied, "but I'm only going up it one way,"

Like my Canadian associate, she laughed loudly and said: "You will endeavour to get me there alive, won't you?"

Following this charade, Mrs Arab personally asked for me on further bookings and I was assigned to her for a month. She was a gracious and friendly employer and I enjoyed her company immensely.

On the final day of my working for her, she asked me to drive her to the Savoy for lunch.

She asked me to wait for two hours, but in the meantime invited me to order a meal for myself and bill it to her slate.

After our lunch, she came down and informed me she would no longer need me to drive her back, as she was staying. She thanked me for my services and hoped we would see each other at a later date. What happened next was uncomfortable in the extreme. Instinctively and certainly unprofessionally, I gestured towards giving her an innocent peck on the cheek.

She recoiled in shock rather than horror I suspect, maintaining the composure of a Shaykhah...which is what she was!

She then apologized and quietly announced that whilst appreciating and understanding our customs, if she was seen to engage in them, the outcomes would be unthinkable...for both of us!

I left her slightly shaken – me, that is – but grateful for the time we'd spent together.

Things got better... well *I* did, just spending time on the 'knowledge' for those few months.

In the last couple of weeks before returning to college, I received a tip from one fare for just looking like the golfer Nick Faldo and then was assigned to the late and great Bob Hoskins.

Bob was a lovely man, a 'WYSIWYG'. After picking him up at Heathrow, where he'd flown in from Ireland on the set of his latest film, I took him to the parked limousine. I opened the rear door for him, whereupon he announced that the car was "fuckin' long" and that he would prefer to talk to me up at the front.

The journey was about an hour to his North London home and with reference to the *Long Good Friday*, I told him that was the best 'Long Good Hour' of chatter I'd had in a long time. We talked about his son Jack who was playing the trumpet and about his recent interview with Terry Wogan.

At the end of the journey, I informed Bob that I had interviewed him for a longer period than Wogan. He laughed and invited me in for "a cuppa".

All was going swimmingly well. I said my goodbyes and then drove off...with his luggage!

To be fair, he was chuckled to bits and was equally understanding when I got him and his family lost on the way to the airport. In response to his wife's legitimate misgivings, he simply said: "He knows what he's doing and certainly knows London better than me."

(*No, I didn't!*)

Whilst I was at Heathrow once waiting for Bob, I happened to catch the eye of a woman who, like me, was waiting for an arrival. I can only describe her as the most beautiful woman I had ever seen. She was a stunning example of the human form and I was almost transfixed if not mesmerized by her natural beauty. I didn't have the courage to approach her, but many years later, when I heard the song 'You're Beautiful' by James Blunt, the words perfectly expressed my thoughts and emotions about this woman at the time.

During the summer of my second year at teacher training, I continued with the VIP chauffeuring and was assigned to the Sultan of Oman's residence at Upper Brook Street near Mayfair and Michel Roux's famous restaurant La Gavroche. The Sultan had a vast entourage of staff, which required no less than twenty limousines from a number of companies. It was made clear to me by the older and more experienced drivers that there was indeed a pecking order in terms of the more lucrative assignments. Like *Strictly*, when the contestants are informed of their appointed partners, I was the Anton Du Beke of the chauffeuring pool and was left with the Sultan's

Hat-maker, Chef and Tailor. I would have preferred Major Maamri of the security services, but it was a good gig.

Part of this contract specified that drivers were to be on twenty-four-hour call-out for five weeks! Subsequently, we were billeted in rooms at the Dorchester Hotel, which was owned by the Sultan. The younger drivers were always called upon first, to carry out menial bring-me-fetch-me errands. On one such occasion, I was called upon to fetch a pamphlet from the Tower of London...at midnight! I appealed to our rather slobbish, overweight 'Fat Controller' that this was a capricious whim of our employer and surely it could wait until morning. He tore a strip off me and demanded that I got out of bed, get dressed and carry out the demands of the Sultan without question. Swearing and cursing at his lack of considera-tion – the Sultan, that is – and the imperious attitude of the 'Fat Controller', I went.

As I had suspected, the place was shut. So, I tried to find someone on duty and eventually collared a Beef-eater, who – guess what? – told me to come back in the morning. I said I couldn't because, like *The Godfather*, the Sultan gets what he wants. After making no ground with this guardian of the crown jewels, I offered him a bribe of fifty pounds! A fortune in the '80s. His eyes lit up like spotlights and said:

"For that kind of money, I'll break into the bloody shop myself!"

He did, and although I was temporarily fifty quid down, I returned with the booklet and handed it to one of the Sultan's household on duty, with my receipt.

Early the next morning, all twenty drivers were summoned to Upper Brook Street to await further orders.

The Sultan was going to his country estate to meet Prince Charles. We were to take his entourage to Marlow for a picnic. Each car was loaded with a sumptuous, alcohol-free banquet prepared on silver platters.

Off we set with our respective passengers. Upon arrival at the preordained destination, we lined up our cars in starboard echelon in the village of Marlow.

All of our dependants (men of course) were dressed in the finest Savile Row suits. The tailor exited the car as I opened the rear door and requested I open the boot. As I did, he reached for a leather briefcase and opened it to reveal the *sole* contents: fifty-pound notes, stacked in one-thousand-pound wads! The case was full to the brim. He then nonchalantly took one single note, closed the attaché case and wandered off in the direction of a Co-op shop he'd spotted.

Several moments later, he emerged from the shop with a Sunblest loaf and a Dairylea wheel. My first impression was that he must have pissed off the cashier, having taken most of her float. He then made his way back to the car, whereupon others in his troupe decided they would buy the same. Whilst in possession of these gastronomic treats, they actually sat on the curbside dressed in their finery and started to eat them. A quick glance at the puzzled looks on the faces of my colleagues prompted me to ask the obvious question:

"What about the buffet in our car boots?"

The tailor merely shrugged his shoulders and said: "You eat it." So we bloody well did!

That wasn't the end of it. The hat-maker had spotted a hat shop. So off he went and soon arrived back with a rather dashing headpiece and cane to boot. They all wanted the same apparel!

Off *they* went and eventually returned with similar garments – all except for a very despondent tailor who revealed that the shop had sold out. He made his way over to me and said:

"You'll drive me back here tomorrow."

I replied that he could purchase similar goods from tailors in Savile Row, a stone's throw from his residence in Upper Brook Street. He was having none of it and was prepared – no, determined – to spend an extra premium to come back to Marlow; much to the envy and disapproval of my older peers. That gave me an overwhelming sense of satisfaction, and the obvious glee on my face clearly displeased the other drivers, not to mention the 'Fat Controller' when I got back. Seething, he said:

"I've already assigned you to some other errands."

"Ooh, I'm afraid you'll have to reassign," I replied.

"Well, get back quickly!" he ordered.

On the long journey there and back, I cooked up a rather brazen and rebellious plan.

On one previous occasion, I had transported Major Maamri to an evening liaison. I had enjoyed his company and we connected well. He trusted me, as I did reciprocally.

The Major had a distinctive voice and I reckoned with a little practice I might replicate it very accurately.

The next morning, I summoned up the courage to call the 'Fat Controller':

"Good morning," and it was – 5.55 a.m. to be precise. I thought our Deployment Officer should be at his desk for his 6.00 shift and I needed to speak to him before our temporary, esteemed employers did: "This is Major Maamri."

"Oh, good morning Major, how may I help you?" said the 'Fat Controller' in an obsequious tone reserved for those paying his income:

"I need to have a driver assigned to me for the duration of this visit and I should like to have the one called Franklin."

"Of course sir, I shall let him know immediately. Is there anything else I can do for you?"

"I will contact you presently."

"Right sir, goodbye sir."

"Three bags full sir," I thought.

I'd only gone and pulled it off! Mind you, it was no great achievement: he was after all, cognitively challenged!

When I arrived in the control room, a flustered controller called me over in his typical imperious fashion:

"Right, Franklin, what have you got on today?"

I told him.

"Well, you've been reassigned to Major Maamri. I'll get somebody to cover those other jobs."

"But, but I've already planned those routes." (My appeal was convincingly delivered.) "Can't somebody else serve Maamri?"

The reply was expected:

"Don't argue, do as you're told and be ready!"

"Get in!" I thought. There are moments when one experiences an overwhelming sense of self-satisfaction, and this was just so an occasion.

The next three weeks saw me transport the Major to a number of liaisons, none of which involved work relating to his official capacity. On one occasion, he asked me to transport him and an escort to a plush restaurant and wait for two hours. His escort, in a detectable East End accent, made a plea:

"You can't leave him out here for two hours. Bring him in with us!"

"A rather nonplussed Major succumbed to her demands and an equally nonplussed driver had his first Thai meal, in an extraordinary, unanticipated event.

I felt that we bonded over the three-week period we were together. When it was time to say goodbye, the

Major was generous. He gave me a very plush Swiss watch and also presented me with something a little more unusual…well, to me anyway. He handed me a small wooden barrel and intimated that the dates within were some of the Sultan's personal store.

I think I hid my initial indifference well and duly accepted this second gift, before warmly parting company.

I'd only ever experienced those seasonal, sticky, 'Eat Me' dates that my mother used to consume and therefore had no compunction whatsoever in handing them over to her.

She opened them immediately and tore open the silver foil seal within; in itself suggesting a quality product. Her face exuded a level of delight that I would never have associated with eating dried fruit.

"Do you know what these are?" she said. "Try one."

I rather reluctantly tried one and a non-sticky delight, with a caramel consistency, assaulted my tastebuds. This was my first ever Royal Medjoul date and to this day have never tasted anything near as good.

As the Sultan took off in his private Boeing 747, the head of the driver's pool handed each of us an envelope. The contents poleaxed us! Each driver was given a £500 tip from the Sultan; a fortune now, but a veritable treasure trove in 1989!

After some considerable thought, I decided not to waste this serendipitous windfall.

I bought a painting by Lou Burnett in Mayfair: a period depiction of the Arc de Triomphe. I almost gaze at it daily, up at its position on our dining-room wall and often recount its origins to guests or family.

Chapter Four

PREPARING AND ACCLIMATISING FOR THE ASCENT

I FOUND the second year of teacher training less daunting, though just as demanding.

The school placements manifested themselves either as daily visits or in blocks of three weeks for the first year, five weeks for the second, or eight weeks for the final year, with graded increases of responsibility, in terms of class teaching.

In the first year, daily visits and the longer placement meant assisting or teaching independently with small groups. In the second, there were limited periods of teaching whole-class lessons.

The planning, preparation and evaluation (PPE) – not to be confused with latter-day personal, protective equipment, which should have been very useful in my day, what with the continuous and innumerable airborne diseases spread by the average child – was lengthy, demanding and very time-consuming.

Incidentally, later, at one of the schools under my leadership, there was a very disagreeable Foundation Stage teacher, with whom I would have numerous differences of opinion. She always regarded her role as union representative as a means of undermining my authority or decision-making within her militant faction; which was counter-productive, as I always believed success in school relied heavily upon consensus. Anyway, I couldn't help thinking she looked a bit like an 'Orc': not the ugliest person in the world, but would have probably made the semi-finals. She always had a look of disapproval, as if one of the children had shit themselves and she'd had been the first to smell it!

On one very significant occasion, a young child had been sick on the carpeted area and when I enquired as to why it hadn't been cleaned up, she imperiously replied: "It's not in my job description!"

I retorted: "Would you like me to put it in?"

In fact, I did indeed make a small addition to all staff job descriptions as a result of subsequent events which just read… "Carry out any *reasonable* task as requested by the Headteacher."

She said, rather insubordinately, that I earned far more money than her and that there must be something in my lengthier job description that covered incidences such as this.

Feeling emotions rising within but maintaining the dignity of my position, I replied that my job description was in fact, shorter than hers. With a look of perplexity and dumbfoundment, she said that it was impossible: mine had to be longer?

"No," I replied, "mine has just two words – 'work' and 'hard'."

Off she strode, but the unfortunate outcome of this delayed, vital clean-up was a serious infectious contamination which affected a significant number of children, resulting in the forced closure of my school by the Public Health Agency who ordered a deep clean.

I had a number of difficult staff meetings surrounding

the important issues of Health and Safety. One notable issue involved the use of 'Epipens'. My Deputy, of all people, said the teaching union stated that staff were not medically trained and therefore should not administer this kind of treatment. My reply was incisive and impassioned, stating that if mine or any of their children were anaphylactic sufferers, wouldn't we want a teacher to save their life by administering an injection? After all, the worst that could happen, if erroneously injected, was a hyperactive pupil. The alternative outcome of a reticent teacher was a possible dead child!

I often wondered how on earth educated people could not see the obvious rationale in certain circumstances, or even think logically on issues or events, which I and undoubtedly many others regarded as 'Day One'! For example, a head cook whom I inherited and who believed herself to be omnipotent, approached me with a sense of urgency, to demand that I shut the school with immediate effect because the boiler had gone down. She said there was no hot water. I had only been at the school a matter of days, so I asked her where the boiler was situated. It didn't take long to diagnose that the pilot light had gone out, which meant holding down the grey button for fifteen seconds and then 'snapping' the red ignition button. I had a similar set-up at home and presumed she must have had too. Nevertheless, catastrophe averted, I went back to the kitchen and explained what she might do if such an event reoccurred. Guess what? It wasn't in her job description! However, my little addendum to hers and everyone else's job description meant that it was from now on.

On another occasion, whilst on one of my daily rounds in the depths of winter, I couldn't help but notice that in one of the classrooms all the windows were fully open! I approached the teacher and asked why. She replied that the radiators were too hot! I sarcastically asked her what her course of action might be, should this have happened at home? Unsurprisingly, she was able to formulate the correct answer. Asking (quite sarcastically again) if she could transfer or re-apply these skills, she angrily replied:

"Am I allowed to touch the radiators?"

To which I replied:

"Yes, in much the same way as you can touch the window handles."

However, back to the classroom-based training. I always felt comfortable and confident with planning for and performing class teaching. In a way and some might say, it was exactly like acting. Clearly, this kind of self-possession was a prerequisite of teaching and not all students had it.

What I felt more challenging was the need to produce better-structured essays for my studied subject areas, if I were to ultimately achieve a 2:1; a non-negotiable personal target.

Rick and Clive English, another post-graduate who I met in the Middle East during the 1970s, helped me enormously and I am forever grateful to them.

Rick helped me more specifically with the teaching elements of my set tasks, having a remarkable insight into 'Behaviourist' and 'Cognitivist' theories and exponents.

Clive, on the other hand, was a geographer and was invaluable in matters relating to my core subject.

What both these doyens refused to do was to 'spoonfeed' me. They insisted on my writing any given assignment and would then give me direction to follow up in terms of improvement. This approach was invaluable in developing both my understanding and ultimately, my argument.

I met Clive in Saudi Arabia in January 1978, whilst on a two-year contract with Hunting Technical and Groundwater Services. I left on the first day of September 1977, to be employed as a mobile auger operator in the desert. I remember the period well, with news of the death of Elvis still resonating in my ears and (as a nineteen-year-old) suffering the upheaval of my roots.

Clive was already a post-graduate and employed as a soil surveyor. We struck up a friendship: a strong bond that has lasted years.

One day, after we had received some much-anticipated communication from home, I noticed that Clive was opening a letter from a relative. The two ends of the written letter 'C' of his name had almost joined up to form an 'O'. It looked as if the envelope had been addressed to 'Olive' and that, consequently, became the name he reluctantly adopted from me. His response was "You pratt!" and has similarly become his preferred greeting to me... on *every* occasion.

Proverbially, I went to Saudi a boy and two years later came back a man.

People often ask me if I enjoyed it out there. My stock answer has always been:

"Yes, for the first six...hours!"

I have many memories, but several stand out starkly against the rest:

On one particular afternoon in April, we drivers had emerged from our tents into the heat and blinding brightness, with cupped hands over our eyes, straining to see the twice-weekly passing of Concorde to and from Bahrain. Although it was five miles up, as usual, the tiny silver dart passed three-quarters of the way through our sighting, before a huge sonic boom shook the camp, as if a large field gun had discharged a shell right beside us.

After the event, we were conscious of a dark bank of cloud on the horizon above the ragged, fossiliferous hills, which had replaced the more familiar backdrop of a clear sapphire sky.

At first glance, we all agreed that it was a sandstorm which prompted us to secure and cover the vehicles.

As the cloud bank got progressively closer, the portent looked far more sinister and foreboding.

The first sign of imminent danger and the onslaught of Armageddon came in the form of trident-shaped lightning bolts that streaked low over our heads, with simultaneous thunderclaps. It was not a sandstorm, but a fully-blown storm surge – a hurricane, if you will!

A wall of rain like stair-rods and hail the size of golf balls assailed us and they bloody well hurt! We ran as fast as we could to the shelter of one of the caravans; drenched before we reached the door. The lightning bolts were blinding and the thunderclaps were concussive.

I saw the power of the wind pick up fifty-six-gallon drums of diesel and send them careering down the slope from the top of the fuel dump...end to end!

The fear was etched into the faces of everyone and all we could do was ride this out.

Before our very eyes, the wind blew over a four-ton caravan which had been secured to the ground with giant, six-foot-long metal pegs. The wind continued to buffet our bolthole.

Within a relatively short period of time, which seemed like an age, we were aware of an acute silence that had descended upon us. We tentatively ventured outside. The first thing that struck us, apart from the deathly silence, was a three-hundred-and-sixty-degree wall of black cloud surrounding us. We were smack-bang in the middle of the eye of the storm! It didn't take us long to realise that we had all this to come again; and inevitably, come again the horror did.

After the storm had abated, we gazed upon the mesas in the distance. Remarkably, huge channels had been exca-vated by the driving rain down the slopes; thus, forming streams in spate. In the middle distance, a mirror-like-mirage flood-plain had formed.

Two days later, we awoke to see an unforgettable and remarkable sight. As far as the eye could see, the desert was awash with brilliant colour. Flowers of all shapes, sizes and colours had sprung up, jostling in the light breeze. On closer inspection, tadpoles were swimming in various-sized lakes and ray-reflecting puddles. Insects were in abundance and birds were performing effortless aerobatics; darting and flitting in their flashing-feathered colours The whole area was alive with wildlife and frenetic energy, against a background of azure and spring sunshine.

We were later informed about certain species of frogs that could hibernate for periods of up to seven years during droughts and then suddenly spring into life after rain penetrated the ground.

The life cycles of flora and fauna had been fast-forwarded like a video in their remarkable colours and mating calls; and then, as quickly as this phenomenon had appeared, it disappeared. The desert once again became a backdrop of semi-arid, sun-tortured desolation.

The next time I had any reference to this memory-moment event was twenty years later, when Will, the head-teacher at my first school, gave his speech at my leaving event:

"He has the ability to make the desert bloom."

We'd never discussed my experiences of this.

However, he could not have known the true impact of his praise upon me, nor indeed I, regarding the impression I must have made on him.

This had been the first most violent land-based hurricane aftermath I'd witnessed. The second had been the notorious storm of October 1987, remarkably dismissed by weatherman Michael Fish.

In the case of the latter, I'd just arrived back at college after attending a two-hundred-year anniversary dinner for The Coldstream Guards.

The difference was, presumably like Mr Fish, I'd been drinking…like a proverbial fish, I suppose, and completely slept through it. Not until the following morning did I see the resulting carnage of felled trees in the grounds or news footage of the national disaster.

The next event took place late one evening after the lighting from the camp generator was shut off. Olive and I had made our way down to the *wadi* for a bathe in the well before retiring to bed.

We were quietly washing ourselves in the silent darkness when at once we became aware of a padded encroachment. To our astonishment a cacophony of slurping noises surrounded us and within moments the water had dropped to a level beneath our credentials.

We looked at each other in disbelief as an entire herd of camels had embarked upon a drinking frenzy. These 'ships of the desert' were still approaching the well in our torchlight as we scrambled out; not in fear (although they can be aggressive), but rather to escape the overpowering stench of their breath and bodily odour.

That wasn't the end of the evening's entertainment: on our way back to the tent, the sky was torn on the horizon by an enormous flash of copper-green light as a large meteorite streaked across the sky. We knew that meteorites were often small grains of rock entering the atmosphere and frictional burning created the flash. However, this must have been a sizeable invader, because the resulting light show was magnificent and enveloping.

I had always suffered a little from arachnophobia, but

never again would I be tormented by or reticent about handling indigenous species in the UK after my first encounter with a 'Camel-Spider'. They are not technically spiders but solpugids. They are about six inches long, but with outstretched legs appear to be the size of tea plates.

One evening, Olive and I were working under generator lighting in the workshop, when suddenly I saw this brief image of what seemed to be a spider scramble up Olive's right leg. I wanted to cry out to warn Olive but found myself completely poleaxed with shock and horror in equal amounts.

Olive was only aware of it as it progressed up his torso and let out a shriek comparable to that of a tortured prisoner, I should imagine. His voice appeared to cover the range of four octaves and would have been momentarily higher than that of a coloratura soprano.

I was still suffering from shock when he demanded to know, in his temporary eunuch voice:

"Why the fuck didn't you warn me?"

I replied that I had been shocked into silence.

"You total pratt!" was his response; thus, taking his endearing insult to its highest accolade.

Another memorable event involved our Camp Leader getting stung by a large black scorpion. In truth, it hadn't helped him wandering around the place with flip-flops on.

As he moved a diesel barrel, a disturbed scorpion punctured his big toe! Luckily, his wife, a nurse by profession, had packed him a morphine kit which he duly administered with a syringe.

That still didn't stop him dancing around all day, like a demented marionette.

I'm sad to say I actually had one humanely dispatched and stuffed by a taxidermist on camp, after capturing it crawling up beside my face on the tent wall! He mounted it on a Rothman's cigarette packet with Arabic health warnings.

Shortly, after having arrived at our second encampment 'Miyah', about three-hundred miles north of Riyadh, I took on the role of 'Camp Co-ordinator'. We undoubtedly, if not urgently, required some decent sanitation, so I set about designing some half-functioning toilets. My idea was to dig a large pit, three diesel drums deep; cut the tops and bottoms out of six acquired drums; stand them on top of each other to form two shafts and then fill back the sand around them. I cut two car-tyre inner tubes laterally, to form seals between the drums, to prevent sand from pouring in.

After finishing this mammoth task, I cut two metal plates with holes in them and placed one on top of each shaft. A chair with a hole in the seat was placed on each plate and then two separate tents were erected above the shafts, enclosing the seats for privacy. This was a major engineering feat that Dick Strawbridge would have been proud of!

This luxurious design was greatly appreciated by all and allowed wives the benefit of their own commode. It was used for months, although the flies did inevitably, take up residence.

When we were due to move on, the camp leader suggested that I make safe the shafts, so that passing animals or indeed humans wouldn't fall in. I could have just filled them, which would have been the logical course of action, but for some reason, I wanted to sterilize the shafts by pouring in petrol…two 'jerry cans'-full in each, to be precise. I then poured a long petrol fuse from the toilets (I wasn't stupid) and then ceremoniously lit it with a cigar. Much more fun!

The resulting explosion rocked the camp (rather like

Concorde) and immediately brought everyone out in the open to investigate.

The effect of pouring petrol down two long, straight shafts and igniting it was tantamount to firing a shotgun and the contents within were expelled with great force. Fossilized turds rained down on us like spent 'Pennies from Heaven'. The whole camp was studded with mini blasts-from-the-past. Everywhere, my besieged colleagues were frantically trying and failing to avoid the 'shit-storm' bombardment, shrugging the remnants of the dropping droppings from themselves.

Eventually, the excitement calmed down and Olive, in a newly camouflaged outfit, came over. His words, resonating in my ears, recalled Pike's forbearance at Captain Mainwaring's repeated 'Stupid Boy' insult... "You pratt!"

Chapter Five

KHUMBU ICEFALL

LIKE THE Khumbu Icefall stage of Everest, my third year at college was quite tricky and ever more demanding.

Although I'd had successful feedback from mentors and tutors regarding my placements, I was beginning to feel the strain of the coursework. On top of this, I was going to have to produce a ten-thousand-word dissertation on a subject I had yet to choose and negotiate the final exams.

I'd carried out my final eight-week teaching practice at a First School called Monksmead in Bridgeford. The head-teacher of this establishment was then John Cooper. He was perhaps the most influential character of my career.

When we first met, he was very gracious and welcoming and I thought this was his default greeting when I held out my hand and he didn't shake it, but merely turned and walked off. I felt a little displaced by his apparent snub, but later found out that he was suffering from a deteriorating 'tunnel-vision' condition. By the time I had arrived on the scene, his vision was extremely restricted and myopic. He knew his way around the school by memory but understandably, any change in layout presented him with a challenge.

John was an accomplished orator and during events at which he spoke, whether to parents, guests, celebrations or retirements, I never once saw him refer to notes.

Everything he said was spontaneous. This strength was one of his greatest assets and certainly one that I tried to emulate in my leadership career. His guidance on many issues was invaluable to me. A great teacher!

I recall as a student helping him to teach PE last period every Friday. I remember explicitly saying once that I couldn't believe it was Friday afternoon again and he replied:

"Yes it is and it'll be Friday afternoon again tomorrow."

This reference to 'time flies' is very poignant as I reflect upon it in my retirement and well worth mentioning to younger individuals wanting to wish their lives away.

I was submitting some well-graded assignments, but after my final practice at Monksmead, I needed to focus on the dissertation. This, I decided, was to be music-based and, more specifically, to look for reasons why most children lose their enthusiasm and eagerness for the subject as they enter their teenage years. This tome needed to be ten-thousand words long and required months of research and data analysis. Producing it was taking its toll on my endurance and literary skills.

I remember most vividly, whilst working at home and feeling exhausted with a serious dearth of patience, my mother knocked at my bedroom door, saying that she'd brought some tea. For some inexplicable reason, I flew into a rage which sent her on her way:

"I said I didn't want to be disturbed!"

There was no excuse for this unwarranted outburst and minutes later my brother appeared.

"Now then, what's this all about?" he said.

"Not you as well, Pete! I'm trying to concentrate."

"Maybe I could help?" He couldn't, but I was still feeling guilty over Mum's exit, so I reluctantly humoured him.

"I'm sorry, Pete, but you can't, so best just to leave me alone."

"Well," he continued: "just explain to me what *exactly* it is you have to do."

"I've got to complete a ten-thousand-word dissertation and I'm struggling."

"Ten-thousand words, eh? That's a lot!"

"Exactly my point."

"But in those ten-thousand words, there are likely to be lots of 'ifs', 'buts', 'ands' and 'thes' and if you take these out, that will probably leave you with only eight-thousand words. Then there'll be 'althoughs', becauses' and 'children', etcetera, which will probably only leave you with a further four thousand to find. That's encouraging, isn't it?"

There was a moment of silence as we looked at each other and to be fair, an amount of incredulity on my part. Then, we both burst into uncontrollable and insuppressible laughter.

The pressure and anxiety evaporated almost immediately as Pete left the room.

Pete inherited his wit from Dad: they were both quick-on-the-draw as it were.

After my mugging, I was having trouble with my senses of smell and taste. I said to Dad:

"You could put petrol under my nose and I wouldn't know it was there."

"You would if I set fire to it!" he replied.

I apologised to Mum, who exhibited a good deal of understanding. Then with a fresh cup of tea, went upstairs and just got on with it!

At this time of deadlines, I was greatly indebted to our Principal's secretary Hillary who professionally and speedily typed out my dissertation on the computer. We had become good friends, not only because I was an older student, I suspect, but also because I'd become quite active in the entertainment circles within the college. She had responded positively to my appeals for help; much to the astonishment and disbelief of my colleagues.

When the final exams arrived, I had been revising for six months, following a well-planned schedule of rotated subject content. Information overload afflicted my brain and I just wanted to sit down and start! In total, there were exams across six days and in that time, I wrote *forty* sides of writing!

In short, I achieved my 2:1, through the help, support and guidance of many people, to whom I'm indebted. Exhausted, but elated, I prepared for a celebratory field trip to Iceland.

Eight of us flew to Reykjavik. Three guys and five girls. Four of the latter had been on my course and one of these had brought her eighteen-year-old sister. As we carried only four two-person tents between us, I tried to work out the sleeping arrangements. Nevertheless, off we went.

Knowing what to expect in the 'land of fire and ice', I invested heavily in the appropriate clothing: particularly boots, weather-proof shells and a one-hundred-litre rucksack.

On arrival, we stayed at paid accommodation overnight and availed ourselves of the open-air swimming pool, which was geothermally heated. We swam and bathed until well into the small hours, as it was still light.

The next morning, we were up early for the journey to the glacier, where we would pitch tents in readiness for the ice walk. We also had the opportunity to visit the famous turf-houses, which kept the Vikings warm: a design that has been used for eleven hundred years.

We left the main road (I say main – it was a single track) and walked to the base of the glacier, where we set up our camp. We then set off and had a lengthy, uneventful but enjoyable ice walk. Upon our return, we relaxed for an hour or so and I went off by myself to the melt-water waterfall to relax. Gazing up at this feature, I was acutely aware of and mesmerised by the deafening sound and the distinctive pattern that the falling water produced. It made me think of the time I visited the London Palladium once, when the final curtain unravelled as it descended. It took me moments to record the event as a *haiku*:

> Inexorably
> The final curtain descends
> Rapturous applause

Feeling a sense of fulfilment, I returned to camp for some packaged rehydrated food: the delight and instant gratification of most hungry students. Although I wasn't expecting it, the night was going to be a long one. Upon my arrival, it had been democratically decided, apparently, that I should share a tent with the guest sister. I have no recollection of her name but for the purposes of this anecdote, I shall call her Sophie, the French derivation from the ancient Greek name Sophia meaning *wisdom* and intelligence; for reasons I shall explain presently.

Firstly, however, we decided to discuss the following day's arrangements, which meant catching an early bus to the coast to hop on a ferry to the island of Heimaey. Having agreed a plan, we then settled down to a game of cards, before getting off to sleep.

Some time later, I briefly left the tent we were all packed in to relieve myself and get some fresh air. Whilst doing so, some headlights in the far distance caught my attention. A vehicle had turned off the road and was headed in our direction. I informed the others, who like me wondered who it could be.

A frenzied planning of action took place, in case, as we

suspected, the uninvited visitor turned out to be malevolent. In hindsight, I could have just given him one of my packets of food.

All the same, we waited until the vehicle drew up outside. I went to investigate and saw a well-dressed man alight from a top-of-the-range Range Rover. He warmly shook my hand and offered me his name. He informed me that he had noticed our camp light from the road and wondered if he could talk to us. I invited him over to the already crowded tent, choosing to follow him in.

After a brief exchange of names and the reason for our being there, he announced his purpose:

"I'm from the Jehovah's Witness movement. I should like to explain our philosophy to you and try and recruit some new members."

What, in the name of all that is holy, were the chances of this happening, so far from civilization? This clearly was a man of conviction and totally committed to his faith.

We furtively glanced at each other with wry grins and established a consensus of approval to his request. After all, we weren't going anywhere; there was no television to watch and above all, in our minds for sure, was the opportunity to discuss the emotive issues of blood transfusion.

To say the discussion was lengthy is putting it mildly! At the end of it, we all must have been breathing pure carbon dioxide. To be fair, the man kept his dignified countenance throughout, but the sheer weight of opposition eventually wore him down.

Unsportingly, I suspect, we all regarded this bombardment of his argument with our passionate views and perceived moral high ground as a means of punishing him for having the temerity to bother us in the first place! I don't think any of us gained much clarification of his philosophy, but he wasn't doing much of the talking anyway!

He left palpably exhausted but wasted no time in his getaway.

Then the night really got interesting. We retired to our respective tents for some much-needed rest.

Sophie cleaned her teeth and then intimated that her boyfriend wouldn't like the idea of us both getting undressed in the tent, so would I mind going outside whilst she got changed for bed? I humoured her and took my leave. I waited outside for approximately ten to twelve minutes:

"Ready... or not," I thought and re-entered the tent.

She was dressed in a two-part pyjama outfit and was just zipping up her sleeping bag.

"I'm terribly sorry," I said, "but I don't think my girlfriend would like you to see me getting ready for bed, so could you turn over?

"Yes, of course," she replied. As she did so, I put extra layers on.

"Ready," I announced. She turned back to say goodnight and performed a double-take!

"You've put more clothing on!" she exclaimed. "Are you teasing me?"

"Yes, that's correct and you'll do well to follow my example. The temperature is going to drop below minus ten tonight and I don't think those pretty flannelette pyjamas are going to prevent you from freezing to death. While we're at it – as it were – would you be greatly offended if I checked your rucksack?"

A little confused, she consented. I then unsnapped the lid and pulled up the extendable neck of the sack. The top third of the bag was packed with *crisp packets* and directly beneath these was a fairly large *make-up bag*!

"Oh my God! Didn't anyone advise you on what to bring?"

"Why, what's wrong?"

"Well, for a start this make-up bag should have been a first-aid kit. These crisp packets have taken up room for proper food (albeit dehydrated) and your bloody pyjamas should have been thermal underwear!"

Close to tears, she asked me to leave the tent for a second time. Upon my return, she was once again, fully dressed and zipped up. Noticing that she had forgotten something, I picked up her woolly hat and placed it on her head.

"You're going to need this as well. I think your boyfriend would approve. Goodnight."

It's odd, how I'd never *really* thought of the ten-year age difference between me and my student friends, until the death of Paul in year one. Undoubtedly, I would have made daft blunders through naivety at their age, but in the case of Paul, it had resulted in his death. Now I felt more like a father figure in their company.

It's one of the strange phenomena of growing older. One is inclined to forget what they were like at a younger age and tolerance appears to be shorter in supply. I once heard Chris Evans on the radio say: "I knew my father was right when my children started telling me I was wrong!"

We made an early start next morning and caught the bus to the south coast. Throughout the journey, I was aware of a frosty (pun intended) reception from Sophie, along with a great deal of gesticulating between herself and her sister.

The ferry trip between the mainland and Heimaey was horrendous! To a person, everyone suffered extreme sea-sickness and a reappearance of their breakfast. Eventually, the waves subsided and we landed on the dock at Vestmannaeyjar shaken and stirred.

Strangely, my first impression of Heimaey Island was not dissimilar from a normal housing estate at home. Nice buildings, gardens and parked cars out front. However, a short walking distance out of town brought us to what can only be described as a lunar landscape.

On the 23rd of January 1973, a fissure opened up less than a mile from the town of Vestmannaeyjar. A curtain of lava, approximately a mile long, was spewed up into the air. The newly formed Eldfell volcano continued to erupt for about six months. It destroyed several hundred homes, engulfing the island with 200 million tons of ash and sending flows of lava towards the harbour, where the seawater was raised to a temperature of forty-four degrees centigrade.

The harbour, although narrower but more sheltered today, was saved by workers pumping seawater onto the leading edge of the flows.

Miraculously, the population of about five thousand, with the exception of rescue workers, was evacuated successfully. Within a year, they would all be back.

Looking at the post-apocalyptic scene, we were stunned to see abandoned homes with cooled lava emerging from windows and front doors! Household furniture could still be seen within.

We found a guide who was prepared to take us up to the crater and impart some of the statistical information and explain the geological features.

As we traversed the cone, the guide suggested we quicken our pace as the residual heat in the cooled lava would melt the rubber soles of our boots. The sulphurous stench was almost overwhelming.

Having taken many rolls of film between us (obviously, we never had the advantages of digital technology), we went to see the famous Puffin population, before returning to the mainland via calmer waters.

The final excursion before flying home was to walk the rift valley between the diverging North American and Eurasian tectonic plates. Incredibly, Iceland is perhaps the only place on Earth where the effects of two major tectonic plates drifting apart can easily be seen above sea level.

The flight home was uneventful, apart from one brain-transplant donor in our party, who tried to take their petrol-filled stove on board…and it wasn't Sophie! We sat next to each other and enjoyed our intercourse, whether her boyfriend would have approved or not.

Chapter Six

HEADING TOWARDS CAMP ONE

THE FOURTH year seemed interminable, as this was my sixth year in further education: equating to an additional secondary schooling. This final year was perhaps the hardest to endure, as most of my best friends had left. I felt as if the parole council had refused me release from prison. However, the end was in sight and the year afforded me the opportunity and flexibility to organise a big show to support my performing arts studies, within the 'Honours' award.

By way of a thank you, I gave Hillary, family and friends tickets to an end-of-term show in which I had top billing. I told her and others that there would be a surprise worth coming to see. I also gave tickets to my new employer William as he and his governors had given me a conditional post to start in the last half-term of the school year. I was unaware that his one other, was not his wife but she who would eventually be mine; his Head of Year Five.

I asked my former 'Bridgemen' friends if they should like to perform a set at the show, to which they agreed. I think they either misconstrued my intentions, genuinely lost track of time, or more accurately felt they should have topped the bill! They were on stage much longer than expected, drawing looks of discontent from my surprise backing group – The Coldstream Guards Dance Band.

Eddie Claxton was our brass band musical director and an outstanding trumpet player. To this day I have never heard anyone play the 'Last Post' so hauntingly or solemnly at a Remembrance Day event. I managed to persuade him and some of his colleagues, with whom I was familiar, to back me for a small fee in transport costs.

Rightly so, they had invited me to London to rehearse, to decide if I was good enough to sing with them. They did, after all, have a reputation to uphold. I think they were pleasantly surprised.

I can tell you now, even after thirty years, the hairs on the back of my neck still stand up, when I recall how they sounded during our set. All accomplished musicians to a man!

When that level of professionalism strikes up behind you, one of two things can happen:

One can feel totally overwhelmed and dumbstruck by the moment, or be elevated to a new level of performance. I felt like a musical celebrity and super-charged with confidence. I even got up and danced with a woman in the front row during the saxophone instrumental break in Billy Joel's 'Just The Way You Are'.

Eddie asked me at one point if I felt confident enough to ask for requests.

"Bring it on," I said. In my heightened state of awareness and inflated sense of importance, I would have sung at The Palladium's Royal Variety Show!

At one point, I was heckled by a drunken student. He had no hope of spoiling my night:

"It appears you possess Van Gogh's ear for music, my friend!"

I simply don't know where that came from, but the audience loved it. He attempted to come back at me. It was then I let him have *both* barrels:

"The last time I saw a mouth like that it was being gaffed into a boat."

The audience and band alike erupted with laughter. So did Alison Moyet who I spotted in the hall... Had no inkling she'd be there!

It was a memorable night that I shall never forget or ever repeat and the concert lasted almost three hours. Short – by Ken Dodd's standards!

Chapter Seven

ARRIVAL AT CAMP ONE

MY FINAL exams finished on a Friday in that June of 1991. I was in full-time teaching employment from the Monday of the following week. Intuitively, I felt confident about the 'Honours' award.

I had but two days to celebrate my achievement. By many middle-class standards, I'm sure this was a common event of average expectations. For me, however, it was an almost insurmountable goal. Yes, I felt proud that I had become the first member of my family to achieve this accolade, but believe me, it wouldn't have been possible without their faith and support.

These newly acquired 'letters' of achievement, eventually found themselves printed on my chequebook; much to the amusement and ridicule of some of my acquaintances. However, even to this day, I value them all the more for knowing *just how hard* they were to secure.

Dressed in my best suit, I entered with some pride through the gates of Broomsgrove Middle School in my hometown as a newly-qualified teacher (NQT). I was filled with equal measures of trepidation and confidence.

I couldn't find the entrance at first and ended up walking round the back of the school, by the kitchen bins. It was here I found an individual who couldn't be more than twelve, smoking a cigarette!

"Put that out!" I demanded, walking towards him.

"Fuck off!" he replied.

In an instant, I concluded that this could be the beginning of a long and illustrious future, or the ignominious end of a prospective career.

I couldn't let this jumped-up cocky individual intimidate me. My time at the school wouldn't be worth living; well not until he left anyway and even then, his power to influence others' behaviour over me would remain. I'm afraid the red mist descended.

I grabbed his fashionably shortened tie and slammed him up against one of the bins; knocking the air from his lungs:

"Wrong teacher, wrong answer, now put it out and don't let me catch you smoking on school premises again!"

I gave him a moment to capitulate and then politely asked him where the front entrance was. He gave directions.

As I entered the building, to be greeted by the Head-teacher, I was still contemplating the possible outcomes of my indiscretion and felt a little displaced with the rush of adrenalin. I wasn't proud of my actions. It wasn't very professional, but on balance I felt it was necessary for my very survival there. Experience was to equip me with more favourable and effective alternatives for the future.

Sean wasn't a bad lad, but his behaviour could be frustratingly disruptive and intimidating to staff and children alike.

Following our encounter, there were, fortunately, no follow-up complaints or the inevitable accountability to parents. I think this is because he abided by a set of principles and ideals that constituted honourable behaviour in his community and acknowledged the new leader of the pack. Contrarily, but perhaps predictably, I got on well with Sean from that moment on. He'd come from a hard background and like anyone, wanted to be understood; just like his brother.

Our unfortunate introduction singularly defined my path of teaching and leadership, in that I consciously and willingly wanted to teach at more challenging schools and 'champion the underdog' as it were. I received far more reward from making major breakthroughs with difficult, unwilling, or cognitively challenged children. It was not always plain sailing though and I had much to learn in dealing with Special Educational Needs (SEN) children.

It's true, I gained a reputation throughout my career for being firm, even intimidating to some, but essentially fair. Moreover, those children who came to know me, understood that there were boundaries not to be crossed, but equally and above all, knew I wanted teaching and learning to be fun within a safe and secure environment.

My first early morning staff briefing was unsettling. So much to assimilate. I felt very nervous and surprisingly under-qualified. Will gave me a huge introduction but there didn't seem to be much of a warm welcome. In fact, I didn't find out, until some years later, that there had been a well of resentment brought about by Will's hyper-inflated opinion of me and my skills, as a direct result of the concert he'd attended.

I caught sight of the Deputy Head, Maggie, who looked unsettlingly formidable, with her extraordinarily long grey hair tied in a ponytail and her stern matron-like gaze. In fairness, I felt like a fish out of water and ironically, intimidated.

In later years I was to evoke this occasion when children moving to the High School regarded change as a threat, rather than an opportunity.

I was assigned to Year Five as a class teacher within this three-form entry school and as an NQT, allocated a full-time classroom assistant with my Year Leader as mentor. This meant frequent observational visits by senior staff...a daunting prospect!

I left the meeting and my acting Head of Year, (Whilst Gwynneth Evans was on maternity leave) took me to my classroom and introduced me to my assistant. She had planned the week's work and gave me a brief outline of Core and Foundation subject objectives.

The morning went to plan and at lunchtime I prepared for the afternoon.

When my assistant returned from lunch, I thought I should involve her in my plan of action, regarding a wall display on the Normans, essentially to elicit any ideas she might have.

"Well you're the teacher, you decide," was her terse response.

Obviously, I didn't know at the time that she had been reassigned, moved out of her preferred zone of work and obviously had formed a biased opinion of me, through Will's 'post-concert, coming of the renaissance' address to her friendship faction.

"Yes, you're right, I need to assume the role of command."

I did just that and assigned her a small group of disruptive pupils that had been flagged up on my briefing list.

"They should keep you busy. Any problems let me know."

We had a productive afternoon, with enough artwork for a substantial wall display.

After school, I planned and prepped for the next day. It wasn't until I arrived home that evening, that I felt as drained as a squeezed orange. This physical and mental condition was going to be replicated over the course of twenty-five years.

By the Friday of that week, Sean was going to earn me some more respect; unbeknown to him.

I was sitting with a group of staff eating lunch whilst on duty in the dining hall when one of my colleagues happened to mention that Sean was sitting with his shirt-tail out; a heinous crime. A debate then sparked off about which one of us was going to tell him to tuck it in.

"Not me," they all declared to a person.

Sensing an ideal opportunity to gain some 'Brownie Points' I elected myself to carry out the task. Leaving the group, I made my way over to the table where Sean was seated and plonked myself down right next to him. He turned to face me with a capacity-filled mouth, looking like a pig at a trough; chewing his food in a manner akin to that of a revolving cement mixer. He was a little taken aback at my arrival and suddenly stopped eating as if someone had thrown a switch. The rest of his small gang transfixed their gazes on me.

"Hi, Sean."

My greeting was returned with a nod.

"I should like you to do a small favour for me, please."

Again, he nodded back once.

"I should like you to tuck your shirt in."

A nod, followed by an adept hand movement and the request was completed.

Almost immediately he got back to the business of masticating his food.

I got back to my table, aware of the looks of incredulity on the stunned faces of my colleagues.

"How did you do that so easily?"

I merely stated that Sean and I had connected and shared an understanding.

It is interesting to note that some years later, I was walking through Sean's home patch one night and my path took me past a sizeable group of late teenagers. As I approached, I spotted Sean, very much animated amongst them. My first impression was to expect deserved retribution but in front of his 'pack' he boisterously greeted me with a "Hi Sir!" and told them to make way.

One of the distinct advantages of working within my hometown was that many of the parents grew up and went to school with me.

They trusted and extended to me their blessing to carry out any action or punishment I saw fit to ensure their children behaved and worked hard in school. Like an honour bestowed, although that's not to say that some of their suggestions were unacceptable, but you have to realise that like me, they came from an age when corporal punishment was the norm. It didn't work for the most part then and it wouldn't now, if it were allowed. I think that's why Grandparents like teachers, by virtue of being in loco parentis use more moderate and reasonable methods of education and to greater effect.

Over the years I've found children to be so amazingly resilient and forgiving. Most have only wanted to be given a voice, listened to with an air of interest and spoken to with a degree of respect; all within an environment in which they feel safe and enjoy.

The last half-term of the school year ended as quickly as it had begun and I truly felt that I had gained a footing in my first appointment.

Chapter Eight

REACHING CAMP TWO

DESPERATELY WANTING to make an early impression, I decided to reorganise and decorate my classroom during the summer holiday. My theme for September was going to be 'space exploration.' I completely covered my ceiling with dark blue paper and backed the walls. It took me three weeks!

I purchased enough variable-size Chinese lanterns for the children to cover with papier-mâché and then decorate to represent all the planets in the solar system. I spent not a small amount of my own money to re-equip the room with scissors and other tools. I was keen to ensure the children would enjoy their learning environment, which I wanted to be the envy of the school.

I mounted the quality scissors onto a shadow board. Everything was to have an appropriate place for storage and I was going to give the children the responsibility of maintaining the appearance of their own environment. Proudly looking at the results of my labour, I left the building with just a few days before the start of the autumn term. Preparation of one's classrooms was always undertaken a week or so before term started, to avoid discolouration of the backing paper by the sun.

The first two days of the term were to be 'Baker-Days' or training days, with time in the afternoon to prepare classes and/or lessons. I arrived early on the first day and went directly to my classroom feeling organised and ahead of the game. As I walked into my room, to my horror, the scissors were missing off the board and some blunt-ended, tired old ones were in their place. I felt vandalised. I went straight to my Head of Year to put in a complaint. She said she would investigate the matter. A while later, she returned with the missing scissors but no accompanying reason for their previous disappearance. I later found out that it was she who had taken them, after returning from maternity leave to find that hers were missing. I eventually got my own back by marrying her!

It took the best part of the first half term to complete the planet and space travel theme through integrated teaching, involving the overlapping contents of different subject areas. For example, the 'Apollo' space programme came under history; space travel under geography; The financial costs and the consumption of materials-maths and of course English, art and music pervaded everything.

To be fair the children loved this project and happily threw themselves into it. By the time the project was finished my classroom looked like a mini planetarium. The impact of this display didn't go unnoticed either. Even a visiting Headteacher, to my utter surprise, made overtures about me applying for her retiring Deputy's job. We both felt slightly awkward after informing her I was an NQT in my first job!

If staff at Broomsgrove held a grudge towards me following Will's over-exuberant heralding of my arrival, then my starting pay grade augmented it. In those days, teachers' wages were on a nine-point incremental scale. Two points were initially awarded for a good 'Honours' degree and one for being an NQT. Then there was an additional one for every subsequent year of service.

For teachers coming later into the profession, one

point for every three years served in the public or private sectors was awarded if the work was relevant to teaching. I had worked for three years in the police service on their civil staff; four years as a self-employed mobile retailer and of course two years in a semi-arid region.

Will said with a signed magistrate's affidavit, I could be eligible for a level-six pay-award. I duly applied for and obtained the necessary document, which subsequently lead to the corresponding wage.

One feature of schools is that factions exist, people talk and classified information inevitably leaks out. Quite often this information when passed on, is distorted, misconstrued and results in misplaced or manufactured resentment.

It's fair to say that older members of staff used to associate a salary rise with length of service, which in turn equated to 'experience'. I have always disagreed with this notion, as some teachers taught the same content repetitively over years of service, rather than review their programmes of study.

Experience, in my opinion, coincides with the ability to do a job and apply skills to teaching that have been forged in other private and public sectors. Management was one such skill.

My goodness, I made mistakes and quite often fell short of my own expectations, let alone those of others. However, I observed and listened to good teachers (my Head of Year Five very much included) and was eager to learn from them; modifying my techniques and approaches accordingly.

I forged friendships with like-minded people. We pooled ideas and delivered on our promises; both curricular and extra-curricular endeavours.

The one strength that I possessed above all others and gained through my past experience was a confidence to address any audience; whether a class full of children, a room full of staff, a meeting of governors and officials, or a hall full of parents.

A combination of sustained hard work and positive results over my first full year incredibly induced the senior staff to promote me to the position of Year Eight Coordinator.

Can you imagine the ensuing bitter resentment of other staff? This was indeed a period of open and hidden hostility, especially from those who had been overlooked or displaced. I think the marginalization I felt, duly prepared me for senior management later.

To think I nearly threw the opportunity away because of the tangible antipathy I sensed.

I went to Will's office where he and Maggie heard my misgivings. I told them I was truly grateful and extremely flattered that they should consider me, but I would have to decline their kind offer. Will asked why with a puzzled look.

"It's because I fear the promotion would cause bad feeling amongst some of the staff."

Maggie looked me straight in the eye and replied assertively:

"So, what you're saying is that you doubt our judgement as well as your own?"

The sharp comment tore through me but more importantly brought me at once, to my senses.

I immediately apologised for my reticence and accepted the post; after all, they were making a bold decision and indeed a sizeable gamble.

I was sad to hear of Maggie's passing some years ago, but I am forever grateful to her for that 'shot in the arm'. We had some great fun up to her retirement and I miss her. It just shows how first impressions can be wrong!

Undoubtedly, she introduced me to the often difficult

and sometimes lonely 'buck stops here' decision-making of leadership.

On the last day before she finally hung up her mortar-board. I planted a rowan tree, otherwise known as a mountain ash, within the school grounds in her honour. It was her favourite tree.

We planted the same type of tree along with my mother-in-law's ashes. Both women were indomitable.

Head of Year Eight was challenging but a joyful period in my teaching career. Yes, the children are full of explosive hormones, anti-establishment and authoritarian methods. That said, tune into their wavelength and offer them success and you have impressionable, loyal, contributing and aspiring young adults.

Older children, especially, can be terribly self-conscious but with the right amount of encouragement, can shrug off their reluctance and generally perform to remarkable levels,

They suffer terribly from conflicting emotions; wanting to be treated like grown-ups but equally welcoming advice and guidance.

Shouting doesn't work, nor do final warnings, especially if they can't be implemented. At this age, choices, consequences and quiet, rational communication are the answers; these and above all, well-planned and *engaging* lessons.

Headteachers have an important role when leading assemblies and it's essential to pitch these well, to capture the attention of the older children, otherwise they simply switch off.

We've all made notable bloomers in front of the entire school and I remember Will naming an introductory piece of music as 'Bolero's Ravel'; an easy slip of the tongue. However, perhaps more comical (I dread to think what I've unconsciously got wrong and not been told about)

was the time he tried to attract Year Eight's attention, by asking for some popular singers' names. I could see the twelve-year-olds mutter their interest and back came some replies: "Michael Jackson" ... "George Michael" ... "Queen", to which Will gave his acknowledgements. Then an individual cried out "M.C. Hammer" to nods of approval all round and Will replied:

"Ah, yes, 'If I Had a Hammer' what a wonderful song!"

At once I detected a feeling of 'Oh no, don't bother, it's a false alarm' spread throughout the group and 'normal service has been resumed.'

A week before the summer term ended, all prospective Heads of Year took an afternoon to meet their up-and-coming year groups. I was looking forward to addressing all three forms along with teaching and support staff. Significantly, it was the very first time in my life that I was going to lead a team of professionals. It was an exciting but also daunting and humbling occasion, that required some thoughtful and reflective moments of planning. I certainly wasn't expecting some events to turn out the way they did that afternoon.

During the lunchtime of 'changeover day,' I had a visitation from a displaced Year Seven teacher, demanding to know why I hadn't refused my position. I told her that she would have to take her argument up with the senior management. in fairness even if I had, she still wouldn't have got my post. Her effrontery was staggering! She was *actually* holding me accountable for her being overlooked and slighted. She told me she was going to contact her, or rather our Union. I don't think it improved the situation much when I offered her the contact number. The final straw was when I suggested she go on more training days, starting with anger management. She really tried to intimidate me, but I'd had enough by now and politely asked her to leave and perhaps "boil her head". She left highly animated and full of promise, not the 'Eastern' type.

Wondering if I just imagined our encounter, I got on with the job at hand. I went over to a small window to let in some fresh air. It was stuck but with a little jiggling I realized the catch needed to be manipulated up and across; something I might be able to use at the meeting.

After herding three forms into one at the meeting, I formally introduced myself and focused on one particular individual; no other than Sean's brother who had taken up the 'top-dog' mantle. I asked everyone in the room who was the toughest, meanest character in the year group. There was a unanimous election.

"Great! OK Luke would you mind opening that window for me?"

He obediently responded, but try as he might, he couldn't budge it.

"Oh, come on Luke, it's only a simple window."

I gave him a few more moments, much to the amusement of everyone else and then I said: "When you can fulfil a simple task like opening that window, then you can answer me back. While you're in my year group you'll do as you're told!"

The rest of the children appreciated that and the staff also gave me a nod of approval. They also gave a collective sigh of relief when I announced that he'd be in my class:

"So, you'd better behave!"

A good start I thought – now the matter of uniform.

I made it quite clear that I was going to be strict on uniform, as well as behaviour and that Year Eight was going to be the flagship of the school.

Uniform is a great leveller and team-building asset. Children always like to push the boundaries on uniform, but I was insistent.

The school brochure clearly stated that boys had to wear dark socks with dark trousers unless doing P.E., when they were permitted to wear white socks. During the '80s and '90s it was considered fashionable for boys to wear white socks with dark trousers; a trend that did not sit well with my aesthetical tastes. These days uniform is perhaps less important.

"Any boy breaking this rule must wear a skirt or enrol in ballet lessons," I jokingly imparted.

The girls enjoyed this levity, but it is probably a phrase you would not hear in the present over-politically correct workplace.

I was a stickler for uniform, because too many well-off children used their modification of dress as a fashion statement, which other children were not privileged enough to enjoy. The ridiculing of one's attire was less likely if everyone wore the same apparel.

Then ten minutes into my address one of the girls became dizzy and disorientated and fainted. Unfortunately, she hit her head hard on the way down with a sickening thud and then went into a fit. Quickly and quietly, I asked staff to usher the children out and call an ambulance. The response from everyone was immediate. I then very carefully placed the girl into the recovery position and waited beside her until help arrived.

The ambulance crew administered aid on site until she had made a full recovery.

I visited her home that night to make sure she was well. Her parents told me she'd had no previous attacks. It was just the heat and stress of change. We agreed that she should not come to school the following day.

In the 25 years of my career, injuries to children were my worst fear. Luckily, there were few incidences of a serious nature such as lacerations to an arm put through a window because of disturbed behaviour. There was another incident of a child running on ice, slipping and ending up in hospital for two days with severe concussion and a blood clot on the brain. It was definitely two days, I sat by his bedside with distraught, though non-blame-apportioning parents, who knew a gritting protocol had been carried out, but that didn't assuage my guilt as head teacher of that school.

It always used to annoy me terribly, when local authorities prescribed what could and could not be included in first aid boxes. I understand the exclusion of tablets with diverse medical conditions, but not such items as 'Steri-strips' that I have used to great effect when sealing wounds. My mantra was always 'engage common sense.'

Sometimes, despite all the precautions one might put into place, fate will deal its worst hand; such is the case of a small girl who swallowed a cocktail sausage in the dining room of another school and choked to death. 'There, but for the grace of God...'

Risk assessments covering every conceivable event (after the well-documented sea-canoeing tragedy) filled volumes of files, but alas, they only covered the predictable. Eventually, stifling bureaucracy and worry, made staff reluctant to lead residential trips.

At the end of Year Eight 'change-over day', a boy called Matthew kindly came to congratulate me on my introduction. He candidly admitted that he had an anger-management problem, with which he hoped, I could help.

My reply was that his honesty would ensure that we'd definitely get on. He left, feeling much more assured that I would give his condition some thought and as it transpired, a later event would allow me to act on my promise...

I particularly enjoyed Middle-School education because it allowed staff to teach to their strengths; not only giving children better quality lessons but also cutting down on planning time. It also afforded more time to engage in a wide range of extra-curricular past-times.

We produced some well-collaborated, outstanding musical shows such as *Joseph and His Amazing Technicolor Dreamcoat* and *Robin Hood*.

We employed outside musicians and artists. Indeed, high-quality artwork adorned the school throughout and we formed a large orchestra. Our upper schools certainly gained from the wealth of talent we moved up.

As Geography Coordinator for the school, I was encouraged to apply for a Mountain Leadership Training Board (M.L.T.B.) certificate, which would allow me to take pupils on residential visits. Although this was to take place over six days during the October half-term holiday, I wanted to do it; not only because it was a prestigious award, but because children could experience the 'great wild outdoors'. Future 'Duke of Edinburgh' applicants benefited from learning map-reading skills. It also enabled me to take adults on 'The Pennine Way' and 'Coast-To-Coast' trails. Great memories!

On the Sunday afternoon at the beginning of half term, I was ready for the trip to Moel Siabod a mountain in Snowdonia which sits in isolation above the villages of Betws-y-Coed and Capel Curig. At the base of this 872-metre peak is the UK National Mountain Centre Plas-Y-Brenin, where we stayed. Twelve of us were on the course and I turned up outfitted with a 100-litre rucksack; the contents of which included those I was asked to bring and others which I kept quiet about, but nonetheless in my opinion, important. I also had a stave well over a metre long and a good pair of boots and gloves.

The amount of ribbing I received (all in good fun of course) had been expected but I'd come more than prepared. Those who chose to travel lighter with 65-litre 'Jaguar' sacks thought I was on an SAS training hike.

On the night we arrived, we had to hit the ground running so-to-speak. At 12:00 midnight, we were all driven to a large, forested area and asked to form pairs with randomly named partners. Each pair was given a map with twelve coordinated points. At each one, a code would be displayed for recording to prove we'd found it. We were timed and had to complete the task in one hour. Time of course was of the essence. Everyone set off at staggered times to avoid 'hangers-on'. We set off and my partner decided that we should locate the furthest coordinates first; running to the first and then systematically ticking the rest off on the way back. A great idea I thought, with less chance of grouping with others on the nearer coordinates. We didn't have our sacks, so our movement wasn't hampered.

The exercise went well and we managed to arrive back first even before the pairs who had left earlier. My partner was competitive and I liked that as we were of similar personalities.

I enjoyed the rope training. Indeed, some of the techniques I learnt I'm still employing today, such as the 'lorry-man's knot'; the emergency lift harness, and 'figure-of-eight'.

On the second night, we had a night-time orienteering test. We didn't know where we were going when we left at midnight. We had to read our maps with head-lamps from the point of leaving and follow the roads taken.

When we arrived we were given a number from one to twelve, so each of us had to lead the party over the corresponding leg of the journey. Obviously, we couldn't use compasses because we had no reference points in the darkness, so were instructed to use the 'handrails' of walls, water and sheep pens illustrated on the O.S. maps. Inevitably, I was given number twelve, so I was going to have to read the map from beginning to end in order to know where I was on the last leg. The examiner said everyone had to keep reading the map because they might ask an earlier leader to orientate again. In reality, this didn't happen.

With sustained concentration and accompanying tiredness, we completed the task. I led the group back over the final leg and we eventually reached a previously erected camp and collapsed into our sleeping bags. I felt cold that night...bloody cold!

This training has always reminded me to keep up with the direction finding on serious walks; particularly when leaders are relying on GPS and digital aids. These of course require satellite communication and more importantly batteries, which inevitably, *will* let you down. The Mountain Rescue Service use GPS for speed and ease of locating climbers and walkers in distress, but the difference is, they can all read a map and compass.

Before our final camping expedition, we had to climb Moel Siabod with full kit, during daylight hours. As I set off with my monstrous sack, Gore-Tex shells and stave, others including the examiners, questioned whether I was carrying too much for the challenging climb. I parried their concerns and continued.

The route was tough, especially above the snow line. At one point, I slipped and started to fall down a snow-covered slope. To my horror, my waterproof trousers were acting like a sledge and the weight of my pack was providing the impetus. I desperately stabbed the ground once with my pole to no avail and then on the second attempt, used all my strength and fear to plunge my pole into the snow and luckily, this arrested my descent. I must have fallen a good twenty metres, but worried onlookers quickly realised the usefulness and effectiveness of that additional item of equipment.

We eventually reached the summit, paused, then very

quickly the weather turned inclement. All at once, everywhere was shrouded in a very cold damp fog, which rendered landmark reference-points useless.

We gathered around a trig point, so knew our position and therefore were able to employ a technique known as 'leapfrogging'. This is where you set a bearing from a point of reference and send a member of your party ahead until they just begin to disappear in the mist. Then they turn to face you and line themselves up to your directions on the bearing… "Left a bit, right a bit', etc. The main party then walk to that person and the procedure is repeated from their position. Obviously, there are obstacles and adjustments that need to be made.

The examiners knew there were some dangerous landmarks and erring on the side of caution decided to delay the dissent in the hope the cloud lifted. At this point, morale like the temperature was dipping. I suddenly asked if everyone fancied a nice hot cup of tea and a Mars bar. The ensuing barrage of abuse was quite disparaging, until I rummaged in my bag and extracted a small stove and fourteen chocolate bars. I requested enough water from each individual and poured it into the stove's cover pan then lit it with waterproof matches.

As the water boiled, I added some tea bags and produced some UHT milk capsules. I then poured the piping hot reviving drink into disposable cups and handed it around the utterly astonished but appreciative team. One of the examiners asked what else I had in the bag. I replied:

"Change of clothes, spare gloves, a rope, some distress flares and a 'Gore-Tex' sleeping-bag cover."

"Noted!" he replied.

Our descent took place in a more buoyant mood with some individuals apologising for their mocking. I couldn't blame them; it was bloody heavy!

On the penultimate evening before our departure on the Saturday, we were each interviewed by the examiners.

"You've had a very successful week Paul, but before we give you our results, we wanted to ask you about that long stave. we know the big sack was justifiable, was the long pole?"

"Well, for every reason you tell me I shouldn't have brought it, I'll give you three as to why I should have. It possibly avoided my being badly injured on Moel Siabod; two people can clutch both ends and carry a person sitting on it with an injury; I've used it to gauge the depth of a stream; ward off inquisitive cattle and horses; use it as a splint; pull others along, or use it as a washing/drying-line post."

"OK enough! enough!" Is there anything you would like to share with us that you feel you didn't get right?

"Yes, I brought the wrong type of sleeping bag. I erroneously purchased a two-season bag and I needed a four-season one, because it was cold up on Moel Siabod!

"We'd like to share our decision to nominate you as best student and examinee of the course."

I felt inflated with pride and success and thanked them profoundly for their decision.

"It was that stunt with the bloody stove that did it, but why bring all that extra clothing?"

"If I'm going to take children on expeditions, I know they'll forget to bring some essential comforts. It's what they do," I said.

Smiling, we shook hands and departed.

What I learned on that course in terms of map-reading and survival tips has kept me in good stead for many years.

At the beginning of the next half-term, two boys were sent to me by another member of staff on playground duty for fighting. Both were in my class and although I told them that I was extremely embarrassed and disappointed, the event had been predictable.

One of the characters was a tall, well-built Canadian lad; the other was...yes you've guessed Matthew, the large 'unit' with the anger-management problem.

"Look, you're both in my class and have absolutely nothing to prove. You both have strengths and I'd rather utilise these than punish you. From this moment on, you're both agents or deputies under my command. Matthew, you'll be my 'left-arm' man and Liam, my 'right-arm' man. From now on, you're going to watch each other's backs and become trusted friends. I'm going to employ you as a force for good. If someone is being bullied, protect and stand up for them. If someone is frightened to walk home on their own, accompany them; especially if they're walking in your direction. Is that a deal?"

Both boys, feeling a little relieved, agreed to the proposals and shook hands. They became great friends and for the rest of the year, seriously made a difference to others' anxiety issues and in maintaining the equilibrium within the year group and indeed the school. I had an extra two pairs of eyes and ears and the combined presence of these big lads, even made Sean's brother think twice.

Yes, on several occasions, I had to curb the tendencies of 'Bruce Banner' to use disproportionate force, but ultimately, he moved on, in greater control of his temper.

Chapter Nine

AVALANCHE

ONE MORNING, in the Spring term of that school year, a member of staff appeared, saying my father wanted to talk to me. Knowing this was unusual for Dad to interrupt me during my teaching, I quickly arranged some cover and went to see him.

He told me that he was driving to a gardening job and his van had broken down. Ordinarily, this wouldn't have been enough for dad to have disturbed me in school. Something far more important was troubling him and as he was explaining the possible causes for its malfunction, he broke down and cried; the very first time I'd ever seen him release this kind of emotion.

And then, he mentioned Kay, my brother's fiancée, who had died several days previously.

Understandably, the minor issues had become insurmountable in the wake of this family tragedy.

Over Christmas of the previous year, we had noticed a significant lump that had appeared on Kay's neck and urged her to have it investigated. It turned out to be Non-Hodgkin Lymphoma.

Despite medical intervention, she quickly, over the course of the year, succumbed to the condition.

I remember visiting her in hospital in the September, on one of the multiple occasions she had been admitted for treatment. She looked racked with pain and discomfort:

"Hi Kay, I've brought you a present."

"Why go through that unnecessary trouble,? There's nothing I need."

I handed her a tin of baked beans with sausages. She first appeared to look quizzically at the gift and then erupted into laughter; the last time I would ever see her do so. She died the following January, within days of her proposed marriage to Pete. We were all at her bedside. I was shocked to see her in her final hours, looking like something out of Edvard Munch's 'The Scream'. We were indebted to the kindness and caring nature of the nurses that had made her passing as comfortable as possible. Oh, how we depend so much on these angels!

Vicariously experiencing my Brother's pain, we all were haunted by this distressful event.

Inexplicably, I was, in Vera Brittain's words (taken from *A Testament of Youth*), elevated to a… 'height of articulateness'. In only ten minutes I had written the following song and later performed it at her funeral.

This Sweet Surrender
You've had a long hard fight
But now you have to go
Had so little time together
To share the love we know
Reach out and hold my hand
I'm here to see you through
This sweet surrender
No more tears to cry
Except for us who stay
There's an end to all the suffering
For those who go away

I'll never leave your side
I'm here to see you through
This sweet surrender
Please Don't wait for me
Even though my heart is breaking
As I look at you and see
All the pain that you are taking
Please don't wait for me
You'll find a place
Where there's eternal love
Now there's no more light
And winter seems much colder
For those you leave behind forever
Each year as we grow older
Our love will never die
We're here to see you through
This sweet surrender

At the end of the Summer term, my family had the totally unexpected invitation to attend the Royal Navy Ball at HMS Culdrose, in Helston, Cornwall. This surprise came from the brother of my sister's boyfriend, Commander Martin Butcher.

Martin had served as a Wing-Commander of a Sea-King helicopter squadron in the Falklands campaign. He was at the scene of the sinking of HMS Sheffield and was assigned to pick up survivors. During this operation, his radar gave warning of an incoming Exocet missile towards his aircraft. Taking evasive action, Martin instantly lost height, to allow the missile to go over him and his crew. After plummeting to a lower level, the Exocet still passed *beneath* them!

What struck me most about Martin, was always his composure. I never once saw him lose patience with subordinates, his children or even us.

Whilst visiting his squadron at Culdrose, he allowed his young son to play with the controls and switches of his helicopter. When I questioned him over this apparent laissez-faire attitude, he merely replied:

"It makes damn sure I carry out a full cockpit check before taking off."

Later as Commander of a minesweeper moored up alongside HMS Belfast, he allowed us on board for a routine trip up the Thames, during which Tower Bridge was lifted.

Not long after this Martin was diagnosed with cancer and sadly died a short time later.

Martin enjoyed our company and the feeling was mutual. He wanted the whole family to attend the grand white-tie and ball-gown event, which comprised a five-course dinner and breakfast the following morning. Drinks were free and the tables were adorned with lavish ice sculptures. The group 'Dexy's Midnight Runners' were commissioned to perform.

With high expectations, I went to Will's office for permission to leave at lunchtime on the final day of term, in order to catch the train from Paddington to the West Country.

Will politely refused my request. Thoroughly dejected, I asked why and his reply was that if he allowed me to do it, then it would mean his setting a precedent and having to 'bend' the rules for others. I respected his decision but didn't entirely agree with it. I had worked tirelessly on projects for the school in my own time. Will sought order and organization within the rulebook and like many Headteachers, adhered closely to the Authority's code.

I do remember him saying once:

"If you ever become a Headteacher, make sure your Governors are informed of your thinking. Get them on board. Wise words, which I never forgot.

I eventually got to the ball much later than I'd hoped and missed the main event. However, I resolved that if I ever got to become a leader, I would put the 'Humanity in Headship'.

Things are not by any means black and white in life and I've learned that if staff are happy in their private lives, then they're likely to be happy in their professional life.

As a headteacher, I insisted on staff attending their children's sports-day, assemblies; open days and graduations. I was sympathetic over funerals and compassionate leave. Traumatic events, such as death in the family or divorce, are bad enough when you don't have to teach and plan.

In the running of three schools over nineteen years, I believe every serving member of staff under me, from cleaners to cooks to teachers and senior management, all benefited from a slight 'bending' of the rules. We are not robots!

I remember one outstanding member of staff asking me for permission to leave at lunchtime on a Friday in order to get down to London to prepare for a wedding on the Saturday. With the memory of Culdrose in my mind, I told her this would not be possible. The disappointment on her face appeared instantly.

"Why?" she appealed.

"Because if you leave at that time, you'll hit all the traffic. Not only that, but you won't have any time to see London properly. I suggest you leave on Wednesday night, if your husband can get leave, sightsee on Thursday and prepare for the wedding on Friday. I'll take your class for two days. It'll give me a chance to get to know your children and see how they are getting on.

Her gratitude had no bounds and upon her return the following Monday, I discovered a bottle of wine and a card on my desk. More importantly, when she became a part-time teacher after raising a family, she willingly came into school on her non-teaching days, if we had an Ofsted visit, or something important was in the pipeline.

I have always sympathised with and vigorously defended, the right for good learning support staff to have a commensurate salary. Higher Level Teaching Assistants (HLTAs) have always been expected to cover absent teaching staff for a fraction of their wage. They are, without doubt, indispensable in schools; often overlooked and generally good at their jobs. I have no compunction in saying I listened to and looked after mine.

I've probably only had two members of staff, in my entire leadership career, who have taken advantage of my generosity, but ended up regretting their actions. In the main, the returns I've received for an understanding and generous outlook are incalculable.

Chapter Ten

THE ASCENT TO CAMP THREE

THE FOLLOWING autumn term saw me experience my first OFSTED visit. I don't think I was too trepidatious at this stage; partially, because of my dealings with assessments and inspections in the private sector, but mainly because I'd never endured one of these.

The change in mood and expectations was overwhelming. People were visibly nervous and worried about the judgements and preparations. Will and Maggie were like 'cats on a hot-tin roof' and their palpable anxiety was meted down to Heads-of Year, who in turn, wielded the 'Sword of Damocles' over those with positions of responsibility.

In those days an OFSTED Inspection lasted a week.

I've 'run the gauntlet' of no less than *fourteen* OFSTEDs in various stages and posts of my career, so do feel able to pass judgement on the process:

Yes, it can be an ordeal, which imposes great stresses on staff, to the extent that some literally collapse or experience breakdowns. Men and Women in 'power dress', sometimes with supercilious, sanctimonious and self-righteous attitudes, armed with clipboards and template-comments, perceivably revel in the task of making judgemental observations of hapless staff.

Some inspectors made the visits more supportive than onerous and looked for strengths rather than weaknesses.

In all, I'd wager that very few, if none, could place themselves anymore in front of a class, and pull an excellent grade out of the bag, so to speak.

My technique was to somehow-willingly or not-involve them in my teaching, which not only took them out of their comfort zone but equally reminded them of the need to multi-task.

In short, teachers who are good at their work, plan and prepare well, will come out on top.

My doubts about the process, involve concerns over 'National Expectations' and algorithms; comparing one part of the country or school with another. The frameworks of these OFSTED visits mutate like the Corona Virus. No two schools or children are alike.

I should say that when Michael Gove was Education Secretary, his 'Capes and Bays' attitude along with a 'one-approach-fits-all' outlook and end of schooling exams, had a damaging effect on the educational system. The raft of antipathy towards his policies would later have him removed from his position and mandate. I would go as far as to say that he singularly and ultimately, destroyed my faith in Government intervention measures. On more than one occasion, I saw his pouting-lipped, trombone-playing, Douglas-like character from the Lurpak adverts, stuck on dartboards in staffrooms.

They're still getting it wrong today, during one of the worst recorded pandemics and he's still in office, despite having shown himself to be a duplicitous, self-interested and untrustworthy individual.

My answer? I hear you say, would be to employ a multi-faceted approach to learning. If children don't learn the way you teach, then you must teach the way they learn.

Children may be visual, kinaesthetic, oral or aural learners. What is for sure, is that they learn through differing processes.

Some prefer modular work and testing, whilst others have the ability to store and regurgitate information when required.

I've always extolled the mantra which promotes teaching and testing to the child.

That said, there's still the matter of accountability for schools to deliver good education.

I would suggest they have more frequent, randomly based visits of a *supportive* nature from their local authorities, with equal powers to invoke appropriate action if necessary. We used to have this arrangement, where outstanding practitioners were assigned to a 'Pyramid' of schools.

Even when I was a Headteacher, I chose to put myself up against inspectors in the classroom to prove that I could 'walk the talk'. Indeed, as my role in senior management demanded, I needed to make routinely organised inspections into classrooms, to make judgements. Teachers were more likely to listen to constructive criticism if they knew I could do what I expected of them. I've been accorded nothing less than 'good' during inspections of my teaching with most of my grades being excellent. I've even had one Chief Inspector make a mock complaint because her findings on teaching had to be re-evaluated from 'Satisfactory' to 'Good' because of my involvement in the timetable.

How on earth can one claim to be a Headteacher if they don't teach!?

One evening during the inspection, I was working in my room planning for the next day, with my cleaner. She was cleaning around my rotating blackboard and commenting on the amount of chalk dust she had to sweep up each day:

"Fascinating stuff, this chalk dust."

"Is it?"

"Yes, I often take it home with me."

"Do you?" (In a 'not very interested, because I'm trying to work' kind of tone.)

"Yes, it's got lots of different uses, apart from writing with on blackboards."

"Has it?" (In a 'please sod off, I'm trying to concentrate, but I'm glad I didn't say that out loud' kind of tone.)

"Oh yes, it prevents silver from tarnishing; deters ants; can be used as a kind of filler on walls; keeps screws secure; put it in locks; stops tools from rusting up; great for removing grease stains and you can put it in hampers for effect."

"That's interesting." (No, I really am interested now!)

"I'm being observed during a science lesson on Thursday. Do you fancy helping me? I'm covering sedimentary rocks. You can talk a little about chalk."

"Oh, I don't think so... I'm not a teacher."

"That's settled then!"

"No!"

"Well, you've just taught me something interesting. Just repeat what you've just told me."

She did and the lesson went swimmingly well.

The inspector was pleased with how I embraced the contributions of auxiliary staff.

When I saw her again sweeping up around my blackboard, I commented on how well she did during the inspection and how she had taught me something useful... like not how to dismiss others so quickly because of time constraints and listen!

"Thank you, but it still doesn't deal with the issue of mess I have to clean up."

"I've heard we'll be getting whiteboards soon."

"Great," she sighed. "It'll be a lot harder cleaning marker-pen ink off the furniture when the kids get hold of them."

To be honest I didn't like marker pens on a shiny surface because they didn't have that frictional value like chalk and slipped all over the place. It was also too easy to smudge handwriting, especially if you were left-handed like me. My shirt sleeves and cuffs used to get covered in ink-washable and indelible.

It was to be another ten years before 'Smart-boards' came on the scene.

Computers were also making an appearance and were the size of monoliths. Gosh, how far they've come in just thirty years!

As a member and euphonium player of the Bridgeford Brass Band, I was asked if I could go to Germany on a town-twinning trip during Oktoberfest. I said it was during school time and therefore, had more chance of becoming the first teacher to go into space. Enter my old 'mucker' Rick who was on the town-twinning committee. He directly approached Will and the Governors, who surprisingly agreed to let me go, as I would be an ambassador with the band, representing the school and town.

Being present whilst Will explained this decision to the rest of the staff, was awkward to flirt recklessly with the understatement again.

The coach drive was interminable and tiring ... mostly for the others, because I couldn't stop talking and joking; after all, I was on 'paid furlough'!

I sat at the back with the other younger players and was a nuisance.

"Hey Alan, (cornet player) what's the difference between you and Radox?"

"I don't know," came the reply.

"Radox bucks up the feet!"

My spoonerism took a few moments to sink in, but then the back end of the coach erupted into raucous laughter and so it went on. By the time we arrived at our hosts' gathering at the Offenburg Fire Station, I was tired, dehydrated and had the mother of all headaches. It didn't help that the Germans had prepared a snack of salted pretzels and beer.

That evening we were invited to a bierkeller a Bavarian-themed cellar bar with wooden benches, a live 'oompah' band and beer food.

By this time, my head had a fissure through it like Heimaey Island. I managed to get a couple of steins down me along with some food, but my condition was worsening.

Then one of my colleagues, Andy – an Irish Guardsman – offered me a 'Resolve' sachet for hangovers and said to try it. I've had them before but was sure that they needed to be taken on an empty stomach. Nevertheless, I was desperate so I 'necked' it with a beer.

Within moments, I felt like a ballerina performing a pirouette. The room started to spin faster and faster until inevitably, Vesuvius erupted! I barely made it to the toilet before re-decorating it! The Resolve tablet exploded inside me, rather like adding Mentos to a fizzy drink, to make a model rocket.

I was in bed all of the following day.

We made lasting friendships with our host families and enjoyed their generous hospitality. Their command of English, to our embarrassment, was very good and exemplifies the saying: "If you speak three languages you're trilingual; if you speak two, you're bilingual and if you speak one, you're British!"

They certainly understood our humour: During a tour around the local area, our guide mentioned that during the war, only one building was left standing after the allied bombing campaign. A colleague's quick response was to say trust The RAF to cock that up!

It wasn't lost in the translation and went down like a John Cleese: "Well you started it!" moment in a Fawlty Towers episode.

It was a long journey back, with most of us feeling like our heads had been assaulted with butter-bats, but luckily, I managed to find the driver's bed located deep in the belly of the coach. The road noise didn't bother me and neither did the other passengers. They welcomed the silence.

At the beginning of the Spring half-term holiday, I was involved in a rugby match. I had played the game since secondary school and even at county level. Whilst at Broomsgrove, I was playing for Tabards, a North London side in Radlett, together with the PE coordinator Keith.

The plan was to play the cup game, after which I'd arranged to travel North with Gwynneth, who had family near my newly-purchased home.

The match was finely poised, with only ten minutes to go, when we conceded a penalty only five yards from our baseline. The opposing side opted for a set piece. We stood alongside each other and waited for the attempt.

The ball found its way into the hands of a front-row forward: a massive unit, headed straight for me. I couldn't tackle his legs, because his forward momentum would take him over the line. I didn't feel I possessed the strength to shift him sideways into touch, so opted to smother the ball. Then, *crunch*, he thrust his shoulder into my chest. All at once, there was a sickening *crack* and an onrush of terrible pain. I must have impeded this player's forward motion by a fraction of a second and he scored. I attempted to play on until the final whistle but was of little use to my team. I wouldn't find out until six months later, that he had broken my sternum or breastbone.

After the match, I asked a teammate to help me off with my shirt. I was unable to wash and could hardly move. Like any idiot, with a strong sense of masculine pride, I chose not to go to hospital but instead have Gwynneth drive me north and drop me off. She expected me to call her before driving back home but I didn't, because I was laid up, incapacitated in bed for a week. On our return journey, I'm sure she must have concluded that I was making excuses and wasn't interested in her but was wrong. It was some time later that I made any overtures to her.

I didn't have any time off work, although hindsight would tell me that I probably should have done so. In actual fact, up until the time I would need a longer period of sick leave, I'd only had two official days off work in *twenty-five years;* both of which, were for Rhinitis operations. If memory serves me correctly, I took marking to both, whilst waiting to be put under!

Months later, I attended a dinner party in Kent. As the evening's jollities unfolded, I found myself wanting to sneeze at the table but consciously held my breath, to suppress the urge to do so. Suddenly, there was a loud *crack* which resonated around the table. Someone commented: "What was that?"

To which I replied: "I think I need to go to hospital."

Someone kindly drove me and I was soon talking to the duty nurse in triage: "When did this injury take place?"

She said: "About six months ago."

"Six months!" she retorted in a sharp tone, accompanied by a contorted face, with an aggressive demeanour.

"Y…yes, I passively replied, expecting her reaction to be one of mock anger, over my tardiness.

"I can't be wasting time on you. I've got people here that are really needing my attention. Wait over there!"

I did...for four long hours in abject pain. Eventually, she came to me as the last patient and reluctantly acceded to my wishes and arranged for an X-Ray.

When the results finally arrived, the nurse came to me along with a doctor.

"I think I owe you an apology," she said. "The results have shown a healing injury to your sternum which has fractured again. You also have two torn ligaments."

I was a fool, I should have had this checked at the time it occurred, for I was later to regret it.

I still got a bollocking off the nurse...albeit this time, a well-intentioned one!

In the spring of '96, I got wind of a deputy post, at a junior school in Stevenage and applied for it. My application was successful and a new path opened itself up to me.

I have only the utmost respect for Gwynneth; not only had she secured herself a degree at night school during the time I was at Broomsgrove, but she was also under pressure to apply for and secure a position further north, as she was coming with me. She had worked for over seventeen years at Broomsgrove. She continued in senior positions at three further schools and would have been an excellent Headteacher, had she not selflessly prioritised the upbringing of our children.

I came to enjoy my time at Broomsgrove immensely. We had good times and made some great friends.

Tim, with whom I'd exchanged some negative comments at times, brought tears to my eyes when he announced in front of a capacity-filled staffroom:

"I didn't like you when you first joined us, but we're going to miss you. You won't get any thanks for taking Gwynneth, though."

Chapter Eleven

CAMP THREE (LHOTSE WALL)

WHEN I mention Peartree Spring Junior School in Stevenage, the name will undoubtedly not conjure up any significance in most people's minds. However, it is the Junior school that Lewis Hamilton, the Formula1 legend attended (*or not as the case may be*) He was certainly very active on the go-carting circuits in his final year, when I arrived for my interview in the March.

When I walked through the main doors, it was apparent that this was an ageing building, that celebrated its heyday back in the late Fifties or Sixties. It looked dark, with its over-polished, parquet hardwood flooring and paucity of light. On the walls were special honours and acknowledgements to World War II RAF pilots and Churchillian quotes; the residual adorations of a former Headmaster.

The incumbent Headteacher John had done much and spent much in attempting to modernise the building, but its inevitable demolition and modern replacement on the school playing field was impending.

He welcomed me and introduced me to the Chair of Governors, (another John would you believe?) who in turn led me to other candidates waiting. There were four shortlisted.

Incidentally, the name 'John' has been associated with

a number of influential individuals and events through-out my working life. When I went to the Middle East, I used John as an imaginary middle name in my passport, because the Saudis wouldn't let me into the country without one.

At the time, my Senior Project Manager was also called John. As I've already shared, I built and blew up a 'John'!

Attending interviews is a gruelling, demanding and tiring experience. They drain your strength; both physically and mentally. When you're not being interviewed, one must afford the courtesies of being interactive with members of staff and children. Polite, social graces are observed amongst the candidates, but these hide a disdain and lack of emotional investment for what they really are-opponents!

We were all given a schedule for the day and I was to be the last candidate interviewed. My performance would have to be good, because more than likely, the interviewing panel would be tired. On the other hand, the situation might lend itself for me to leave a lasting impression at the end.

Throughout the day, including lunchtime, I attempted to visit all the teaching staff. I knew they would have a voice before the final decision was cast. By the same token, I'd be able to glean some information about the school leadership from them. Some staff just can't help venting their spleens on such occasions.

I had a plan! After responding to an interviewer's question, I was going to ask if I'd sufficiently answered their question; thus, disarming them later with the disappointing phrase: "Well, I'm afraid you didn't answer the question fully."

By the time I was called, soundbites were whizzing around in my head, like a snowstorm. I was going to expand any answer with as much relevant detail as possible, to cover all bases as it were.

The main interview went well, I thought and then the Chair of Governors came out with a very strange question:

"If you were part of a jigsaw puzzle, what part would you be?"

I paused, and let that one soak in. It was likely that previous interviewees would have said things such as:

"Oh, I'd be a corner piece, pulling people in." Or…

"I'd be right in the centre of it all."

It needed something more impactive.

"Have you almost completed a jigsaw puzzle, only to find there's a single piece missing and you're ecstatically pleased when it turns up? I'm that piece!" Sniggering ensued.

After answering my planned questions (always a good thing in any interview) the chair finished off the interview, by asking if I had made any significant observations of the school, during the day. Well, I thought, he'd asked me a daft question earlier, so I'll give him a reciprocal answer:

"Yes, when I arrived early this morning, there were six rolls of toilet paper in the gents and now there's just one. There must have been some nervous candidates!"

The Head sniggered and later intimated that my… 'bloody cheeky' comments, swung the decision to employ me for everyone.

Will very kindly gave me a number of release days to make the transition easier.

Gwynneth applied for and obtained a post in Ware; a brave move after being at Broomsgrove for so long. She played it down, but the Headteacher at her new school, Pat, knew the calibre of the teacher she appointed.

We found a beautiful Tudor house in a town called Gamlingay, just inside the Cambridge border. We paid the asking price. We were the first to view it that day and agreed it wouldn't be available if the next couple saw it. Like any prospective home, I do believe, instinctively and intuitively, one knows when it's the right one. This was the old mediaeval town hall, with its beautifully fluted wooden beams and enormous inglenook fireplace. Its dining room was an old animal enclosure that dated back to the fourteenth century. It creaked and groaned in the wind, but so do I now! It wouldn't pass building regulations today, but has outlived many and will outlast more that have. The one downside...? It had a bath designed for *The Borrowers*.

I threw myself into Deputy Headship. I had a wonderful class and in that autumn term of '96 decorated the classroom, literally from floor to ceiling with the children's African project work. It certainly impressed our visiting OFSTED inspectors that term (out of the frying pan and into the fire routine). I had only just come through another at Broomsgrove before we left. What great timing! I didn't know it at the time, but if we consider OFSTED to be traffic lights, I was going to 'hit red' on every leg of my educational journey. Rather like people who have multiple attempts at passing a driving test, I was never going to come out of 'inspection or examination mode.'

I was coming to work early, before John and leaving after him; not getting home until late.

This went on for some time until one day, John summoned me to his room. He was sitting down with one of those metal fire buckets in front of him filled with water:

"Watch very carefully," he said... "and comment on what you see."

He dropped a pebble into the water:

"There, what did you see?"

Puzzled, I explained that on impact with the water, the

pebble sent out concentric circles, or ripples of water and after a short time, everything became calm once more.

"Exactly."

"Exactly what?" I replied.

"That's how long it will take the teaching profession to forget you if you drop dead with exhaustion. Now go home earlier to your loved ones."

How right he was!

"The flame that burns twice as bright, burns half as long." (Another Lao Tzu quote)

"We still refuse to listen to our forebears…" Sigh, "*Plus ça change…*"

We chatted at length until suddenly, he let rip a very loud, long, twelve-second, variable-toned fart that reverberated throughout his room. I let out a howl of laughter and took it as a cue and challenge to try and beat it. We took it in turns, as if we were battling it out to win a championship trophy. A short while later, fighting back tears, he said:

"Stop it, stop it! It stinks in here and someone's going to come in and I'm going to have to blame you. I've got my reputation to protect."

We got on famously and worked well together to bring about the changes the school required. For that reason, it came as a shock to learn that he would leave by the end of the school year, to take up an Inspector's post on the Isle of Wight.

In the May of the following year, Gwynneth and I got married at quite an unusual venue, but one which resonated with our pasts.

John benevolently, allowed me two days' compassionate leave, for us to prepare and leave for Malton in North Yorkshire.

We were to be married at a Manor House in Malton, before the wedding party of twenty-four would set off for the breakfast and celebrations aboard The North Yorkshire Moors Railway.

It was a fabulous experience. Our party was contained within one of the Pullman carriages at the rear of the train, which repeatedly, went up and down the line.

We spent our honeymoon at Goathland, the quaint village of TV's *Heartbeat* fame.

When we got the bill for the catering, we questioned the cost of wine for which we had a sale or return agreement. I knew we hadn't drunk it all. Nevertheless, we paid up and agreed it was well worth it. Sometime later, we found out that my Dad had taken some back with him for 'safe-keeping.' You can take the man out of Bridgeford…

By the end of the academic year, it was too late to put the 'wheels in motion' to appoint another Head, so the Governors agreed to promote me to Acting Headteacher.

During the summer holidays, as with tradition, the British Aerobatics Champion Mark Jefferies invited all the residents of Gamlingay to his airfield at Little Gransden for a display. This kind gesture was by way of a thank-you for all the 'noisy inconvenience' of his close-proximity practise flights.

I'm sure some residents must have complained, but we thought it was a privilege to have a world champion go through his paces over our rooftops. And if we thought that was a privilege, then what awaited us as we arrived, was truly special.

His airfield was a comfortable walking distance from our home and just as we arrived, a Mark V Spitfire flew low over a hedge to land on the grass airstrip. We followed it in and chose our place to view the events, which happened to be next to the fuel tanker.

As we cast our eyes over the veteran aircraft, involved in the display, the Spitfire taxied its way over and parked right next to us! The South African pilot jumped out, strolled over to the tanker, picked up a refuelling hose and came back to his aircraft. To my absolute astonishment, he plonked the nozzle in my hand and said in a 'Seth Efrican Eccent': "Fil err rrrup pleeze. Itz a lekker day!"

We spoke at length and that's how I knew it was a Mark V.

He reminded me of 'Sailor Malan', one of our greatest air aces of WW II.

The pilot stayed with us until required to perform. The show was categorically spellbinding.

Our resident aerobatic champion knew just about everyone in the display business and had even arranged the Battle of Britain Memorial Flight, to divert to his airfield, on route to another show.

There were Harvards, vintage, light and aerobatic display aircraft...and the list went on!

What a kind, thoughtful and munificent man. Thank you!

Chapter Twelve

CAMP FOUR: THE DEATH-ZONE

WE HEARD of the death of Princess Diana on the Sunday before I was going to take up my post of Acting Head-teacher. The desperately unhappy and downcast mood of the entire nation was almost tangible.

As I entered what used to be John's room, for the first time in my career, I felt alone, ill-prepared and apprehensive; rather like a high-ranking chess piece, sent forward without support.

Teacher training doesn't prepare you for this. The 'scaffolding', training and support structures were no longer there. I'd only been a Deputy for one year!

Notwithstanding, after the initial shock of near 'ultimate responsibility' I immersed myself into the role; invoking Friedrich Nietzsche's adage that… "What didn't kill me, would make me stronger."

My secretary, who had been at the school a considerable length of time, under multiple Heads, was sympathetic and actively supportive in the major issues of financial probity.

She also took care of the mundane, day-to-day minutiae.

My first consideration was to meet up with the previous year's Head of Year Five, who was Senior Teacher and now taking over the two forms of Year Six as Acting Deputy.

He was a kind, quiet and self-assured man, with a great deal of experience and advice; rather like a sergeant in-the-field. We worked well together and I ensured he had enough release time to perform his management role, outside of his requirement to teach the core subjects.

In any case, I was going to provide teaching support, where my leadership role allowed me.

Two non-pupil preparation and training days helped me enormously to mobilise staff and plan immediate events and draw up an annual events calendar.

I was too busy to worry about my being up to the task and soon settled down into the routines of the post. I took action on the urgent matters first and then gave attention to the important or essential elements of any given day.

Getting on top of the Budget was a major consideration. I decided to give each subject or department coordinator their own devolved responsibility, which not only increased their accountability but also allowed me to concentrate on contractual matters.

I went to regular briefing meetings with the Local Education Authority and had a Mentor Headteacher who helped enormously.

It didn't take long to convince myself, that I was not only up to the task but also going to make damn sure I made an impression or go down fighting!

I encouraged parents and governors to come in and help voluntarily, take on minor responsibilities within classes and organise events – a real community school!

Geraldine came to visit on day release for some weeks. We grew up together as neighbours. She was a beautiful girl of Irish descent. I truly loved her, although she didn't know it at this time because I don't think I could have stood the rejection.

I wrote a song in my teens which I sang at her funeral. However, we used to walk to school and back on occasions and for me the crush or love in the relationship remained unrequited.

She used to wait years before making contact, but when she did, it was a pleasant surprise. Like Nigel Lawson, who named three of his daughters Nigella, Horatia and Thomasina, her father must have desperately wanted boys. Lawson gave up on the fourth with Emily, a bit like Geraldine's father who gave up on the third, but even Veronica has got 'Ron' in it!

I rather like the name Gilbertina but my wife settled on Laura Caroline. I'm not sure my son is so happy with Harrietta.

Here she was now, training to be a teacher and specialising in Special Educational Needs.

I was more than happy to give her a placement. Her kind demeanour ensured she would make a great teacher.

As the weeks grew into months it was clear to me that the worst part of being thrust into headship too soon was behind me. Now I had my eyes on the summit.

I was receiving good reviews from parents, children and Governors and was really enjoying my meetings with construction engineers over the design features of a new school.

It was an exciting time in my life. We were expecting our second child and I was getting on top of my work, although the biggest problem I had, was the need to work smarter by which I mean 'Specific, Measurable, Achievable, Realistic and Timely.

My first school development plan was a tome and it didn't really address accurately enough, the issue of data analysis on child assessment. I was confident on matters of expenditure and wasn't afraid to take calculated risks; even on budgets up to and beyond one-million pounds.

Eighty per cent of any school's budget is preordained as staff salaries. Subject coordinators' expenditure on the children is a minuscule amount by comparison.

I'm naturally economically minded (having lived in Yorkshire) and in eighteen years as a Headteacher, did not once go into the 'red'. Yes, it's easier with a bigger school and budget, but I was still going to have to 'think outside the box' during my tenures.

By the time we reached the end of the spring term, I was genuinely beginning to feel that I would be offered the substantive post. Then the biggest shock and feeling of betrayal was delivered. The chair informed me that they were going to appoint another experienced Head for the September. I knew this had been on the recommendations of the local authority, but although governors have greater control over school matters, rarely do they exercise this power. I appealed to John to overturn this decision, but he didn't and I started to look for another school.

When the new Headteacher arrived in the September of '98 I felt rather marginalised.

I knew that she had to establish her own mode of working and I wasn't now fully on board with all of her decision-making. It wasn't her fault, it's just that my heart was no longer in it and I needed to find a school of my own.

It took four attempts, with one of them being as deputy head in a school in Netherthong, West Yorkshire, very close to my house.

'PowerPoint' had come onto the scene and I went armed with the technology to the interview. It was a good interview – too good. Even when the Chair of Governors asked what I would do if the incumbent head suddenly became ill and was unable to be there. My confident reply involved sending her a get-well card with some flowers, assuring her that things were under control. This prompted a wave of laughter from the panel, but not from the Headteacher.

When Gwynneth asked me how I had performed, I was convinced that I had got the appointment. When I finally received the call, the news was disappointing and deflating.

The Head said I shouldn't be looking for Deputy posts but needed to look for a headship of my own. She was right of course and so I did.

I was due to visit my new school before taking up the substantive role, just as Peartree was due to be demolished and people were moving their belongings over to the new building.

My head was visibly disgruntled and displaced when I announced that I wouldn't be there to help. I eventually left Stevenage with little consideration, but not before I had lifted all of the peripheral hardwood parquet flooring from the old school Hall. It still, to this day, covers the floor of my old dining room. If Lewis Hamilton wants to visit part of the old school floor, upon which he sat, then he's more than welcome to come.

Chapter Thirteen
THE SUMMIT BID

THE INTERVIEW for the post of Headteacher at Donnington Middle School, Oxfordshire was undoubtedly the hardest of my entire working career. Held over two days, it incorporated every conceivable aspect of the job. It wasn't going to be an easy gig. Apart from having to stay at a hotel for two nights, the school was in 'Special Measures' (even more, regular OFSTED visits) and had multi-faith and language considerations. Indeed, the school boasted seventeen different nationalities and twenty-two different languages. Behaviour was out of control.

I drove to the Hotel on the Sunday night, to be sure of a prompt arrival the next morning, but nothing prepared me for what I was going to witness over the course of this ordeal!

There were no fewer than eight candidates for this post; quite a number, but clearly the Governors and Local Authority, wanted every opportunity of selecting the right person.

I arrived on site with three other candidates, just as two were leaving:

"Rather you than me mate...all yours!"

The party entering, looked at each other, gulped, shrugged their shoulders and went in.

As I came into the entrance hall, the temporary Acting

Head John – yes, John again – Rickerson came out of his office and walked down the corridor. As he did so, a rather large black girl from Year Eight, shockingly and disrespectfully, plunged her hand into his hair and cried:

"Hi-ya Rickers, how's it going?"

This single act of dissension was the catalyst for me wanting to get that job. it wasn't the disrespectfulness of the child per se, but rather the system that had allowed her to become so contemptible in her actions.

This wasn't the only act of woeful disobedience we saw, but it became the fundamental and pivotal reason for change in my bid for the post. I distinctly remember mentioning at some point that no effective education can take place unless the shortfalls of poor subject content and control of any lesson were addressed.

Hardly anyone, apart from some of the younger children, was wearing regulation uniform; on the contrary, most were wearing jeans and other casual wear.

After informal introductions, the remaining six candidates were handed interview, teaching and meeting times, as well as a mountain of administrative tasks. Outside of these was perpetual interactions with staff and children.

Some classes I entered appalled me. There was a lack of authority and discipline, which evidently, to a great extent, was attributable to poor teaching. I didn't intervene at this point. This needed some serious consideration and I wasn't going to concern myself until I was offered the role.

I was invited into a science lesson and asked to comment afterwards, in a formal meeting with the teacher and an advisor from the Local Authority.

The lesson delivered to a Year Seven class was good, as indeed was the discipline. I guess this was mainly down to engaging practical work. Having been asked what I might improve, my point of reference was the class's exercise books. For although some of the content was neatly presented and well structured, I wondered if it duly challenged the age of the children.

This comment palpably rankled the teacher; displayed mostly by facial contortions but it seemed to agree with the advisor's findings, who diligently scribbled down my comments.

The Music and Design and Technology lessons I observed were lamentable and delivered by the same egocentric and inadequate tutor. His brief (I use the word advisedly) consisted of his arranging the class in a huge semi-circle and talking for twenty-five minutes. I acknowledged the pupils' strength of endurance and suffering, for most of his address was on behavioural instructions and tool or instrument use. His worst mistake was to give the most disruptive pupils pitiful and unmotivating percussion instruments.

When I mentioned my observations to an advisor she replied: "Good, well you're a musician so he can observe a lesson of yours tomorrow. Let us know what you need."

Not quite what I'd expected but a totally reasonable outcome.

At the end of that gruelling and exhausting day, I was presented with a copy of the school's budgetary dilemma, as well as having to prepare for my main, Governor and pupil interviews.

The music lesson needed to be impressive.

Four of us returned the next day, after two candidates were released – probably a blessing in disguise for them.

I was exhausted, after having read the depressing accounts and preparing for my 'masterclass' lesson, which was to take part just before lunch with a notorious group.

I requested fifteen keyboards, of which five had to come from the local upper school. If you want children to be musicians, then you must allow them to be one. Then off I went to my pupil-led interview.

Interestingly, though not surprisingly, the main issue of debate was behaviour. Many of the pupils felt insecure and in some cases, frightened over the lack of discipline. I said if I was to become the new headteacher I would make it my priority.

Next, the lesson. I asked the children to get into friendship pairs; that was well received. This is a perfect way of relaxing the class and achieving control. The brief introduced the notion of producing two-bar or eight-note jingles to be associated with a product they wished to sell, such as: 'A Mars a day helps you work rest and play.' Simple and achievable. Even if the children couldn't play their keyboards, they could operate them one-fingered and explore the varying sound effects on the synthesizers.

I purposely worked with the children who had been identified as the most disruptive; perfect for proving my philosophy that engagement is the best form of behaviour control.

One young girl, who was potentially troublesome, asked me if she could play on the keyboard, as if historically it had been used as leverage for her compliance.

Her eyes lit up with delightful expectation. Whilst she was experimenting with this normally 'out-of-reach' facility, she wasn't punching some passive victim in the mouth! Furthermore, any chance of a successful outcome might prove to be influential on her behaviour and beneficial in advancing my career. With some help, her partnership came up with a jingle and strapline:

"Cascade shower gel, the one to buy."

The completion and recognition of this task brought a smile and dare I say, an element of shyness, to the applause received; on her part, not mine. The hardest part of my test was to come. By lunchtime, only two of us remained.

Inevitably, the issues of the budget and discipline were to be discussed at length during the interview. When asked how I might address them, I brazenly replied:

"By sacking the worst and highest paid teachers and employing younger, more impressive and talented staff, could we achieve both."

That went down well with the Governors and advisors; not so well with observing staff.

At the end of the interview, I was asked by one of the panel, if anything had struck me as significant during my visit:

"For once, coming to a school where the Chair of Governors looked younger than me!"

The old flippant, throwaway comment came to my aid and went down well. I left the school drained but resolute that I'd given my all. The result was going to be delivered the following day, to help Governors and advisors to debate and allow the two remaining candidates to complete their long journeys safely.

The positive phone call came the following evening. I was elated at the news of securing my first substantive post but realised only too well, that the main issue of discipline at the school had to be resolved. There was also the issue of where to live to consider.

We looked around Oxford for a suitable home, but they were either out of our price range or in unappealing areas. The estate near the school was infamously notorious.

We decided we'd move to my house in West Yorkshire with a young Harry and Laura and Gwynneth would concentrate on looking after the kids and put in for some supply work; a selfless decision. I, by the same token, would take up temporary accommodation in or around Oxford and commute to and from work on a weekly basis.

I was due to take up my post after the Easter holidays and so decided to visit an old friend of mine from the Saudi Arabia project.

Ken was a laboratory technician, based in Riyadh, who I used to visit when I returned to base on leave from camp. As we approached Christmas in 1977, he asked me if I was going home for the festive period. I said no because I was likely not to return to complete the contract.

He replied that he was going home to get married and would return with his newly wedded wife.

I left him with my best wishes and said we'd probably meet up again in the desert, if he could arrange some leave to do so.

Months later, I received the message that he was coming to visit our camp along with his wife and a new auger-operator called Ian. When that day arrived, I came out of my tent in typical, uncomplimentary desert 'toggery.' To welcome the party. I embraced Ken and then watched in anticipation as his wife emerged from inside the vehicle:

"Geraldine!" I cried; simultaneously in disbelief and happiness! What were the chances? Quite high actually: we both lived in Bridgeford; Hunting Survey were based in the same town; and Ken worked for them – just like my father.

"Paul!" she uttered incredulously, though whether that was through unexpectedly meeting me or my transient, vagrant-looking appearance. I'm suspecting it was the former, because she'd already tolerated a long journey, sharing the same vehicle space with Ian!

It was great to see her but made me terribly displaced and lonely when she returned to the capital. Not to worry, I still had Olive and Ian for company, so I would be suitably distracted.

Visiting Ken in his home years later, I was to turn to

him for help over the business of school discipline. I told him that I was going to have to make a big impact on the school, right from the beginning because I didn't have time to settle the discipline problem over time.

Ken was a black belt in Karate and I asked him what the chances were, of me breaking some tiles in front of the children and staff. It didn't matter if I couldn't go through all the tiles I aimed to shatter. I would merely say to onlookers that I would set myself a goal of achieving it at the end of term, in much the same way as they too, would set themselves personal goals in various subjects and disciplines.

Ken raised my hopes and expectations by saying that I was a 'big bloke' and could easily achieve my aim, with some 'tricks-of-the-trade' and the notion of... "Looking at a space beyond the tiles," he assured me that if I placed the tiles on bricks spaced far apart, it would cause a weak spot in the centre of the tiles. Then with enough belief and force, arrive at a place 'beyond the tiles.' He then advised me to practise at home during the holiday. I asked him if I could borrow one of his outfits along with a black belt for greater theatrical impact and he kindly agreed.

Upon my arrival at Donnington at the beginning of the summer term, I was feeling a little trepidatious but intent on my charade going to plan. I met with the Deputy and instructed her that on no account was anyone to meet with or attempt to talk to me until the entire school met in the hall for assembly. I requested that apart from Governors (some of whom might turn up) I wished to see *everyone* associated with the school in the hall at that time; cooks, cleaners, voluntary workers...the lot! When they were all assembled, she was to come and get me.

At precisely 2.00 pm, came the knock at my office door. As I opened it, the sight on my Deputy's face was enough to tell me that I had already made an impression.

I followed her out, down the corridor and into the hall.

To be fair, I thought the sight of me in that dress would stun people into silence, but as far as the children were concerned, it had the opposite effect.

One child cried out: "Oooh, it's the Demon Headmaster!" ...a reference to a current television programme.

Inwardly, I was outraged; not by the inferred reference, but by the mock-terror with which he delivered his comment.

"Not frightening enough for you eh?" I thought; feeling indignant and slighted, if not wounded at the sting of his comment and lack of apprehension. This charged me with added strength as I walked to the table at the front of this noisy congregation.

I removed the cloth that I had previously placed over the six tiles straddling the carefully placed bricks. There was absolutely *no* way I wasn't going to go through them.

As the cacophony of sound increased and the jeers began to crescendo, I took an exaggerated bow, stood up and released an almighty, blood-curdling yell! At the same time, I thrust the palm of my hand down and through the tiles with all my strength. Shrapnel filled the air. Travelling some distance, it hit the windows and landed in the laps of children and staff; narrowly missing faces and exposed limbs. Younger children in the front rows cried with shock and fear and even staff and other onlookers gasped momentarily.

I didn't feel a thing, I was numb with surprise myself, mostly from having fulfilled my intention.

As I slowly raised myself, back up to a standing position, I was at once aware of total silence throughout the hall; even that little mouthy individual had shut up. My first words uttered were:

"Today, I want to talk about discipline; not only about

obeying rules or the expected code of behaviour but also having the strength of mind to succeed."

I went on to say:

"Karate...it means empty hand, but just look at the power of body and mind."

More stunned silence.

I continued by saying that by the next term I was going to set myself the target of breaking eight tiles. (I knew I could already):

"Each and every one of you will set yourself a target in a particular subject that you will attempt to achieve by the same time."

I went on to say that by the following week every pupil would be wearing school uniform. There would be no exceptions. Those that wore Shalwar Kameez and other permitted cultural dress would have to observe the school's colour code.

I told the children that from that point in time, every pupil would say 'Good morning or afternoon' to a passing member of staff and expect a similar greeting in return.

Everyone would say 'please' or 'thank-you' when making or receiving a request and children were permitted to inform me if staff didn't participate. I also wanted to see pupils and staff open doors for each other; be thanked for the courtesy and reply with 'you're welcome'.

In fact, much later, an impressed H.M. Chief Inspector would comment on how this 'impressive' behaviour was obviously instilled and couldn't be performed entirely for the inspection team's benefit.

Finally, I told the children to go home and tell their parents what they had witnessed and to make sure that they complied with my wishes. I added that if any of them would like to come and *talk* to me, that would be permissive, provided they didn't turn up at school in an aggressive mood, because I could be *more* aggressive.

I asked them to leave the hall silently and make their way back to classrooms. As the Deputy Head passed me, she happily thanked me in a relieved tone.

The last member of staff to leave the hall was a slim, diminutive woman called Zara with a warm and kind demeanour. As it happened, one of the better teachers.

"Hi, Mr Franklin."

"Please call me Paul."

"Hi Paul, I've been going to karate classes for more than seven years. I'm a brown belt and I've never seen a technique like yours. Would you mind coming to my club to give a demonstration?"

A slight moment of panic gripped me:

"I should be happy to some time or another, but I fear I'm going to be busy here for a while."

She agreed and left.

For the next day or two, I had to walk around with my right hand permanently in my pocket, because it had come up like a balloon. I rang Ken to tell him how the staged show had gone, but also to ask if he suffered the same discomfort after training. He replied:

"Didn't you place a towel over the tiles before striking them?"

"No, why?"

"Well, we always do!"

The following Monday *every* pupil came to school in permitted and appropriate uniform and there was a perceived and tangible feeling of calm within a more relaxed atmosphere.

Chapter Fourteen

TOP OF THE WORLD

THE FOLLOWING week, after attending a Heads' conference, during which a colleague commented on the 'expertise' of my martial art, I was heading back to my digs. I drove into a self-service garage to get some petrol and went inside the building to pay. As I was doing so, my attention was drawn towards a poster and the front page and headline of a local newspaper:

"Demon Headteacher arrives at Donnington."

I glanced up at the cashier, who similarly looked at the evening edition and then back at me, rather like the woman who recognises the character Tom Hanks plays at the end of the film *Bridge of Spies*.

"Is that you?"

"Yes it is."

"Thought it was… Eleven-fifty, please."

I bought three copies.

Unbeknown to me, the chair of Governors had invited the press to my first assembly. My fake reputation as a qualified martial arts expert now preceded me. It wasn't to be the last time in education, that I would perform, using my superior talents as an actor!

My first week at Donnington saw me bedding down each night in a student accommodation-like hotel on some business park. To say it was basic is rather promoting its status. It was a grey box room, with no television and no other people. When I spoke of this to a teaching colleague at school, who didn't look too dissimilar to Maggie, she informed me of a friend who was looking for a lodger. His name of course was…John!

John's place was in the small idyllic village of Eynsham, just outside of Oxford. We got on tremendously well and I'm not exaggerating when I say that he certainly made my time away from the family that more bearable.

John introduced me to Oxford and his preferred locals. We even visited the theatre several times and accessed a few art museums. On one occasion went to see the travelling show *Stomp!* These visits inspired me to use some of their ideas and techniques in Music and Art lessons.

My office at school was almost self-contained. It had its own toilet and archive room. Whilst exploring the latter one day, I came across some old ledgers and attendance registers which went back to the thirties. Perusing the old records, I came across the name 'Ronald Barker' and discovered that this famous and endearing comedian was an old alumnus of the school; another tenuous link to the world of fame.

My first task as headteacher was to visit every class and teacher. As the school was in 'Special Measures' there was a need for me to make judgemental observations and these would have to coincide with the findings of 'Her Majesty's Inspector' or H.M.I.

These inspectors have far more power or 'clout' than the average OFSTED official. Indeed, they have the potential to close a school down with immediate effect, if they deem it necessary. When they advise on what aspects of change need to be carried out, be assured they must be achieved. They can impose great stresses on the lives of Headteachers and Governors alike. They want, no demand to see change.

I had read the most recent reports and desperately needed to increase the percentage of 'Good' or 'Excellent' teaching. I had some outstanding teachers, who I paired with improving or failing staff for mentoring. Along with my senior management, we set up a rota for the latter to observe good practice, which meant giving their non-teaching periods over to training time. It mattered not, they put up some protest; my job depended upon them carrying out theirs well, so there was no negotiation.

When competency procedures are imposed on a member of staff, it is incumbent upon them to respond positively to training and advice. The correct procedural route must be observed by both parties, which inevitably leads to tears and uncomfortable 'Union Representative' meetings.

The way I used to approach any case, was simple – present facts and indisputable evidence, dispassionately! Union representatives were paid to defend their members, so in some cases had a difficult task. Quite often they would advise failing staff that their prospects were poor without improvement.

I took no satisfaction in seeing staff resign, often jumping before being pushed as it were, but these children were being let down and deserved much better.

The next six-monthly visit from the H.M.I. brought an encouraging report. We weren't out of the woods yet, that would take another two visits, but targets had been achieved and teaching was improving. He was extremely impressed with behaviour and uniform and wondered how on earth I'd managed this over a few months. Little did he realise it had been achieved over the period of one afternoon!

One Sunday evening, whilst travelling back down to Eynsham from West Yorkshire, I became aware that I had not packed any underwear. I called Gwynneth to request that she send me a few pairs down in a jiffy bag. This she did, addressing the package to 'The Headteacher, Donnington School...' without the addition of 'Private and Personal'.

You're probably ahead of me. The package didn't come to me personally but was opened by a rather surprised secretary; one of three to be precise, with whom she insensitively shared the contents. The next thing I know is that Jane, in an act of discreditable and wanton abandonment, if not betrayal, photocopied my underwear and pinned multiple duplicates on the staffroom walls!

It's impossible to relate to the reader, the depth of my embarrassment; not merely because of this invasion of my most intimate apparel, but because they weren't exactly NEXT hipsters.

Oh no, Gwynneth had managed to pick out and send, remnants of a battle-worn wardrobe that should have been burnt and buried years before. Instead, I was faced at every turn with this humiliating view of 'Grandpops' Y-fronts!' And that wasn't the only embarrassing moment that Jane had instigated:

Just before the end of term, I was giving out the usual achievement awards to pupils. Jane had given me a lengthy list of pupil names, that I sometimes struggled with, because of their pronunciation. Notwithstanding, I duly concentrated and was thankful when I got to the last name, which I read out with the same conviction as those preceding it.

"... and finally, last but not least, Hugh Jarce!"

As soon as I had uttered it, I realised that Jane had set me up...again! The whole school burst into raucous laughter and she was almost falling off her seat with mirth. I started laughing too, for the children had to see that I was human after all and besides, it *was* funny.

The provision of Special Educational Needs was indeed a priority on my list, simply because it was in the report of the H.M.I.'s next visit. So, I signed up myself and my SEN Coordinator to attend a workshop, led by a forerunner in this field. He was an Australian called Bill Rogers and was not only very funny but motivational. He came up with methods of alleviating the monotony and finding relief from what he called:

"DADADABD...Day after day after day after bleedin' day."

It was Bill who taught many to avoid possible confrontations, especially with deep-seated problems, by treating individuals like a 'horse-whisperer' would. Make a calm and polite request and turn away to allow 'take-up' time for the child. If this didn't work, then the alternative was to offer choices and consequences. Quite often, it would mean having to endure disagreeable outcomes like missing breaks, but the investments of time were inevitably worthwhile.

I commissioned Bill to present his workshop at two of my schools and although one or two individuals baulked at the cost, it was money extremely well spent.

At the end of the second H.M.I. visit, the inspector pointed out that he had to fail the music/technology teacher because he turned up late for his lesson, leaving unattended children to become disruptive.

This member of staff was difficult to manage, to say the least; not just because he would 'step back from the brink' so to speak, by fulfilling (albeit temporarily) targets set over a given time period. Although I had good reason, I didn't have enough proof for the need to sack him, so I tried another tack: I refused to give him an annual pay increase, based on OFSTED's findings. By hitting him in the wallet as it were, I managed to make more progress;

especially when I applied the word 'sustained' to his reports.

On one occasion, I received reports of a large man of Asian extract, patrolling the corridors. I set out to find him and luckily found him turning the corner towards my office. He was a big unit!

"What are you doing here?" I enquired:

"Fuck off, I'm trying to find a twat!"

Oh dear, I thought, this could be embarrassing. I decided to employ my new 'horse-whispering' techniques.

I said: "Follow me," and turned towards my room, gesturing with my hand, hoping he would comply.

He did. As he entered my room, I closed the door and pointed to Ken's Karate suit that was still hanging up.

"What's that?" I enquired.

"A karate outfit...I've heard about it."

"Do you notice the colour of the belt?"

"Black."

"Good, then you'll know that if anything kicks off in here, one of us will be taken out on a stretcher...and it won't be me!"

There was a stand-off moment and then the man said in a conciliatory tone:

"I'm sorry I swore at you."

"Please sit down," I said... "Would you like a cup of tea?"

"No thanks."

"You're clearly worked up about something. Who were you trying to find?"

"That twat...sorry that idiot of a music teacher. He's always picking on my daughter and I know you'll defend him."

We had more in common than he imagined.

"Well, that's not strictly true, but we just can't go around metering out our own justice. If you tell me exactly what upset you, I'll promise I'll investigate and report back."

The relatively small issues had become cumulative, but they were all 'grist-to-the-mill'.

He left my office less agitated and grateful for the audience with me.

The outcome of not getting smacked was worth the £2000 I'd spent on Bill's workshop and the proximity of my en-suite toilet came in useful too!

Bill's methodology taught me much and proved that time given to parents (and indeed children) to calm down in a comfortable room, with a cup of tea and/or a biscuit, was effective in helping to defuse moments of incendiary behaviour.

In the early autumn term of 1999, I was approached by my upper school mentor, a dynamic headteacher by the name of Ian, who informed me that the Local Authority was organising a trip to The University of Georgia in the States, for Heads to exchange ideas of teaching practice. Thinking it was during the October half-term I declined as I had not seen enough of my family. He then went on to say that the trip was being organised over two weeks including the half term, but we could fly back after a week in time for the break.

It seemed too good to be true, but with the Local Authority's and Governor's blessings we went.

Landing at JFK Airport, it was my first trip to the 'Land of liquid cheese' (as Stephen Fry calls it) and the custom queues were outrageously long. Hours later, when we eventually got to the officials, they were as miserable as hell. Not only that, long periods of sitting down, eating and not exercising, meant that to a person, they all looked like the obese passengers on board the starship Axiom in the film *WALL-E*.

"Hi," I said in a tired and fatigued state. No reply was forthcoming:

"You look like someone's told you a joke and you've already heard it."

As the words left my mouth, I immediately wanted to retrieve them…too late!

"So, we have another Limey wise-cracker. Where's your ESTA, pal?"

"My what?"

"Your ESTA, my overseas comedian. It's a travel authorisation, without it you can't come in. You should have completed it on board the aircraft."

He looked at me with a facial expression of glee; the type you'd expect from a card-player laying down a winning hand.

"Oh, this card. I haven't filled it in yet. I'll do it now."

I clearly brightened up his day, for his sober countenance instantly changed to a child's playground sneer.

"Well do it over there buddy and when it's completed, re-join this queue…at the back!"

I saw Ian on the other side, an hour later.

"That was a good impression you made on that guard. He must have appreciated that."

We hailed down a taxi to get us to the hotel. As we got in the cab, I expected some stereotypical, Brooklyn-based 'Nyew Yawker' to take us to 'Toidy-toid Street'.

I was wrong. Instead, we were greeted by a rather more familiar though nonetheless jolly Asian accent.

We eventually made it to our hotel. Other colleagues had been there ages and invited us to join them on an evening trip to the city by subway.

Tired but happy to go before our trip to Georgia, we dumped our belongings and walked to the subway. Upon arrival, I went to the desk to get some assistance and buy tickets, just as a commotion kicked off outside the building. After purchasing the tickets, I went over to the entrance where the rest of the group were:

"What's happened? What's that large group of people over there?"

"Someone's saying there's been a stabbing."

"Stabbing!?" I cried.

"Welcome to New York," said Ian.

The rest of the evening was spectacular; a meal out, a trip up the Empire State Building and a walk around the bristling, bustling 'City that never sleeps.'

Standing on the eighty-eighth floor of the Empire State Building, looking down at the city through the projecting suicide net, made me think of the great Jimmy Cagney quote from the film *White Heat*:

"Made it, Ma! Top of the world!"

The youngsters will have to look that one up!

Waiting for a cab at twelve-o-clock midnight in Brooklyn, was a sobering experience though and one I would not like to repeat. The eerie sensation of exposure and foreboding was horribly unsettling. The two ends of this trip certainly highlighted the more unsavoury side of this wonderful city.

The next morning, Sunday, four of our party managed to find and persuade a taxi driver to give us a tour of New York for sixty dollars. Before we set off, we asked him to take us to a local diner for an authentic American breakfast. None of us finished it!

He first drove us through Hoboken; a New Jersey city on the Hudson River, famous for being the birthplace of Frank Sinatra. Then we went to Fifth Avenue, Central Park and downtown Manhattan to see the 'Twin Towers'.

Looking up at these internationally recognised landmarks from the front doors, the height and upward perspective, appeared to bring them together at the top. Two years later and the world would witness one of the worst cases of terrorism in history, involving these buildings. I'm transported back in time, whenever I see footage of that terror and can only fall short of imagining, the abject fear experienced by those involved.

I returned to the scene of that horror with some of my closest friends from South Africa in 2016, to pay our respects at the 'Ground Zero' memorial. The three-thousand names inscribed around the basement areas of the North and South Towers are a solemn and terrifying reminder of the grand-scale murder and size of these skyscrapers.

We left JFK that afternoon on a connection flight to Hartsfield-Jackson Atlanta International Airport. The aircraft was much smaller than I had expected; accommodating just one-hundred passengers. I am a notoriously bad flyer; often recounting the reply by Billy Connolly when told... 'When it's your time to go, it's your time to go':

"Yes, but I don't want to go when it's the pilot's time to go... plummeting into the ground like a fucking dart!"

Sitting down in the cramped cabin space, I was immediately put at ease, when I saw our single, flight-attendant. She so reminded me of the... 'jolly hostess selling crisps and tea'... providing us... 'with drinks and theatrical winks...' from the 'National Express' song by The Divine Comedy.

She was wonderfully unattractive, with teeth missing, over-weight, ill-fitting clothes and an... 'arse... the size of a small country' but she was so entertaining with a fabulous personality.

As she delivered the safety procedure movements, to the backing of a pre-recorded tape, it seized no less than three times. At the final, failed attempt, she ejected the tape and threw it into a bin liner, giving a simultaneous, dismissive hand gesture.

I knew the flight was going to be fine, from then on.

Being small, the jet did get buffeted by turbulence, but this lady was always on hand with a kind 'gremlin' grin and curled sandwich and I loved her for it.

Upon landing, we were greeted by our hosts, who looked after us admirably.

The itinerary was to include a day trip to Savannah during our short stay, but we would spend much of our time observing or swapping teaching styles and content within the university and a local middle school. It was very informative.

During one lunchtime I decided to pop out quickly and buy a pair of trainers in order to do a spot of running. I found a supermarket and quickly caught sight of an assistant. I asked if she had a pair of American-size thirteen trainers. She immediately replied in a slow, lazy-sounding southern drawl: "That's purdy, curd ya sayh that agin?"

So, I obliged her.

She then asked me to repeat it a third time, which began to test my patience a little: "I've only got a short time before I have to return to the university, I'm afraid."

She then enquired: "Arr ya from Inglan?"

"Yes I am."

"Lordy! Mine if arr git mah kin?"

She came back with some relation or friend and we performed the same conversation, all over again! Then she introduced another working partner; repeating the process until I had a respectable audience. I eventually got back to the university with my trainers, over an hour later, having been introduced to half of the supermarket workforce. Their excited behaviour, over such a minor event, can only be explained as characteristic of an isolated and unconnected people.

I found my group in a large lecture hall being spoken to by a university tutor. We were sat in a row along a bench, looking at a video-call screen, linked to another university hundreds of miles away. An impressive piece of kit at the time. Then in an act of grinding banality, each one of the visiting Heads was invited to say who they were and where they were from. By the time we got to the tenth person, it was apparent that our captive audience was giving up the will to live.

I could visibly see eyelids closing. By the time it was my turn I said that I wasn't a headteacher. I was an emergency plumber called Paul and I was there to mend a leaking radiator. That broke the monotony and forced one or two of the listeners who'd fallen asleep, to ask what all the laughter was about.

As you'd expect, the Americans were light years ahead of us in terms of technology, but even their middle schools were oppressive in behaviour management. Armed officers roamed the corridors, which had red lines for the pupils to follow, as in prisons (hence, the Johnny Cash lyric: 'I walk the line') and the interiors had no windows, to encourage children to get to their classes quicker. There were distinct parallels between our teaching methods, such as interesting subject content delivered in a motivational way, becomes, in itself, a behavioural management strategy.

That afternoon, several of us visited the local town of 'Franklin'. I noticed that cars parked on a garage forecourt had the town's name punched into their license plates.

With the excitement at the supermarket still in my mind, I decided to try out my accent on the garage owner and share the coincidence of the town's name being the same as mine.

It worked. I came away with the gift of a numberless name-punched license plate… result!

We ate out in a diner that night and it was plain to see why Americans have an obesity crisis.

125

There are no such things as small portions. It's either 'large', 'extra-large' or 'call an ambulance'!

Despite the ridiculous 'tipping protocol' they do at least put water on the table, without having to be asked for it.

Savannah is an interesting coastal city. Behind its beautiful façade of *Gone with the Wind* houses and neatly laid out public squares, is a history of savage slave labour and bloody battles. It is the oldest and largest town in the State of Georgia. It also boasts to have the 'First African Baptist Church' which dates from 1777 and was given to President Lincoln as a Christmas present in 1864, by General Sherman.

On River Street, as you would expect, right next to the Savannah River, visitors can still see warehouses and holding pens which confined slaves.

On the west side of City Market is Franklin Square, which was designed in 1790, in honour of Benjamin Franklin who was an agent for Georgia, whilst in London (hence the ubiquitous references to my namesake and my use of his name-spelling as the opening gambit of many of my introductions). He of course also helped draft the 'Declaration of American Independence' and was a prolific inventor. For me, anyone mad enough to want to fly a kite in a storm, to prove that lightning is in fact electricity, must be a related ancestor; especially, when you consider my methods of sterilising a toilet in Saudi.

All in all, the visit to Georgia was immensely beneficial and opened my eyes to a number of technological innovations, that desperately needed to be introduced into my schools, which in a relatively short period of time I did; utilising a loop-hole in the budgetary allowances.

Even before 9:11, I admit, I was frightened by the lackadaisical attitude towards airport security in the States. True, flights were treated like bus rides, but I was rather concerned when just *asked* if I had packed my own case, rather than have it searched. Answering "yes" was enough to have my luggage taken to the cabin or hold.

I could imagine potential terrorists being asked the same question and replying:

"Oh, most definitely!"

The whole laid-back affair made for a long and uncomfortable trip back.

Chapter Fifteen

SURVIVING THE CONDITIONS

ARRIVING BACK at Donnington for the second half of the autumn term, I was aware that as a whole school, we needed to be fully prepared for what I hoped would be the third and final visit by the H.M.I. Behaviour was very much under control and although teaching had improved dramatically, there was still some distance to go.

Mentoring was the way forward and we increased the time for developing staff to observe colleagues with a proven record of good practice. We used more non-contact time to achieve this and it didn't go down too well. I had joined the teaching programme and had to plan outside of school hours, so I was unsympathetic. Moreover, our climbing out of 'Special Measures' was dependent upon a willing application and endurance. If successful, I could reduce the pressure for a while.

I stressed that careful, planning preparation, self-evaluation and assessment were the key elements and that staff should know their children's requirements.

One day just before lunchtime, a relatively new, younger male member of staff, brought a recently registered girl with 'behaviour and learning difficulties' to my office.

"What's the problem?" I asked.

"She keeps running and hiding under tables and won't come out."

"Have you shouted at her?"

"Yes, but she won't respond to my directions."

I told him to release her for lunch, because I had an urgent need to talk with him…in private.

"Have you read her file and background notes yet, as I suggested to your Year Leader?" I enquired.

"No, not yet, I haven't had time."

"Well, make some time during lunch, because she's a Bosnian refugee, with shell-shock, who's been raped!"

I understood his emotional disbelief and retraction and reassured him that I would help, by assigning a one-to-one support assistant. Teachers are always under pressure to complete a daily set of onerous tasks and communication is vital in the educational process. I was as much to blame for not speaking to him directly. After all, he was a young teacher with great prospects and consequently worked hard to successfully bond with that child.

This child was just one victim in so many disturbing cases, that I would discover throughout my career. One involved a wonderful young girl, who had witnessed her Father murdering her Mother!

As I've already stated, children have a most amazing resilience and deserve to grow up in a healthy, enjoyable environment, where they feel safe and supported. For these reasons, I've always abhorred bullying and will vehemently protect the interests of the victim, especially when parents have threatened to remove their child from school.

On more than one occasion I've had to resort to exclusion, or even permanent exclusion, to defend the rights of the sufferer.

It's *always* been necessary to look at the background of the bully, for in most cases they've been the victim in an upbringing where physical aggression has been the norm. In my entire career, I have met just two children from two different schools, who I would consider to be nasty rather than afflicted; mostly the result of being overindulged or terribly spoilt!

The H.M.I. returned in the spring of the following year. I placed myself in the firing line once again, wishing to be observed along with the staff. In addition to my teaching responsibilities, I felt I needed to deliver a powerful assembly, in order 'to get off on the right foot' as it were. I therefore invested in Bill Bryson's help; not personally but an extract from one of his books... *The Lost Continent*, I recall.

With the entire school in attendance, I started my assembly in the main hall. I had organised some pupil dancers to perform a piece to the musical accompaniment of Sting's 'Desert Rose', which is a perfect fusion of Western and Middle-Eastern styles. That choice certainly satisfied the multicultural elements of the inspection.

I then went on to ask the children if they could remember the first day they attended our school and if it was memorable for them; if so, what could they remember? After several brief conversations, I put it to the children that their day most definitely, wouldn't have been as memorable as James Meredith's.

I drew a parallel between our city of Oxford and the City of Oxford in Mississippi, on an overhead projector, where the university of the same name was located and the one in which Meredith enrolled in 1962.

By the end of the first day, huge rioting had led to the death of two students and multiple cases of injury to police officers, because James Meredith was the first African American to attend the University of Mississippi and the Governor didn't think he had the right.

President Kennedy sent federal troops to escort him through the entrance.

I ended the assembly, by asking the children how proud James or Dr Martin Luther King would be if they could stand where I stood, looking at the success of our multi-cultural school.

That assembly carried some emotional resonance; not only with the school but also with the H.M.I. from whom I received a nod of approval.

During the morning I followed this up with a successful and engaging Geography lesson with Year Eight.

Throughout the day I was receiving snippets, of success from the feedback of passing staff.

"Dare I to dream," I thought.

At the end of the day, The H.M.I. confirmed that we were out of Special Measures. I could have literally hugged him but retained a modicum of dignity.

After his visit, the immensity of relief, went around the school like a 'Mexican wave' and after a period of well-earned celebrations, we eventually settled down to a more familiar routine.

One morning after the holidays, we had an irate parent come into the entrance hall. He couldn't gain entrance because of the security door I'd had fitted, but he was nonetheless, in an aggressive mood. Swearing and cursing at the office staff, he insisted on seeing me:

"I don't care if he is busy, get that twat of a Head-teacher out here now!"

Jane came to the hall where I was teaching and asked if I could come to calm him down. I told her that I was busy and that she'd have to deal with it. When she got back to the entrance hall, the visitor was not in the slightest, put off by her message. Again, he became very irritated:

"Look I'm not leaving here without a meeting with that

complete idiot of a Head. He's done nothing to help my child."

Despite, her protestations he was insistent and continued to rant.

Back came Jane to say that the situation was deteriorating but I was not going to let an angry parent override our appointment protocol. I sent her back and carried on teaching.

Back at the office, other staff were having no success in assuaging this man's anger. One of my secretaries said she would have no choice but to call the police. This threat did nothing to deter him, if anything, it made the situation worse. He threatened to kick down the door and go looking if they didn't bring me to him.

Once again Jane came to the hall; she could see that I was cross, but arrived in a state of discombobulation and visibly shaken.

"Alright," I said, comforting her… "Get me some cover and I'll return with you this time."

She quickly sourced a member of staff and we then went back to the office together.

To her horror, I went to open the security door.

"No, leave it shut and I'll call the police."

"Don't worry, I'll soon deal with this" … and opened the door. "Hi Dad, are you being a nuisance again?"

"Afraid so, son. Are you well?

We embraced each other as the realization of the incident became apparent on the faces of the onlooking staff.

"You bastard!" Jane cried, looking at me and then turning to Dad repeating her profanity:

"Mr Bastard to you, show some respect for my father. Remember my pants and Hugh?"

Chapter Sixteen

OXYGEN

IT WAS great to see Mum and Dad (Mum had waited in the car.) I had invited them down primarily, to see my school for the first time. I know they were proud of my achievements. The time spent with them after a tour of the school afforded the time to reminisce. We spoke about the time when, as a young lad, I helped Dad on his gardening jobs.

Dad for many years had worked nights; it paid better money and he had five kids and a wife to support. Before that, he had 'cut his teeth' as a gardener-cum-landscaper for Odhams Press in Watford.

When he came home from his night shift, he would often tell us stories about the high-jinks he'd become involved in at the Sun Printers, such as passing a short length of hose under toilet doors. The anxious occupants would squirm from side to side in an effort to dodge the expected torrent of water they thought was coming and then dad would throw a bucket of water over the top instead!

On another occasion, he passed a large industrial-sized padlock through the buttonhole of someone's new coat and locked it. When the owner came to put it on, the weight of it nearly pulled him over.

He once stopped someone from pinching his sweets

without asking, by placing foil-wrapped laxatives in the bag!

He had a close black friend in the print and one night whilst they were cleaning their hands, Dad flippantly said:

"You're going to have to scrub your hands harder than that, to get them like mine!"

His friend came back with a withering, humorous reply:

"And you're going to have to work a lot harder to get yours like mine!"

They had a great 'Love Thy Neighbour' relationship; all right for the time perhaps but certainly politically incorrect today!

When I asked Dad if these people ever got their own back on him, he said they tried very hard, but he was always on 'high alert.'

At weekends, my brother and I would laugh along with Dad as we drove in his old Bedford Dormobile to the various gardening jobs in Edgware and Chorleywood.

I remember vividly, how hard Dad worked; in fact, how we all did to help make ends meet.

Sweat used to poor off Dad's brow and the house-owners would always get sixty seconds' worth of distance run from him.

Some used to exploit him terribly and drive down the hourly rate. At one lawn-laying job, he was paid five shillings an hour, or twenty-five pence in today's money.

One employer even asked him, if he was the type who took two hours to complete a job when one would do!

I got so cross one weekend that I said to my father: "One day, I'm going to pull this family out of the gutter!"

It was an inappropriate use of the hyperbole, but nevertheless, a remark borne out of a genuine feeling of despondency.

When Dad found alternative employment, he gave me

his gardening jobs. The first thing I did was increase the hourly rate by fifty per cent. I had lost them all within a month and cared not a jot.

You would be amazed at the change in people's stuffy, middle-class condescending attitude, when they find out you're a teacher, let alone a headteacher.

All five children had their own designated weekly tasks to do, to help around the house. One of mine was to clean *every* pair of footwear over the weekend. Each one of us would put all our shoes, wellies and sportswear into a large egg box (the type that would hold twenty-four trays) and dad would place it outside in the garden for me, so as not to create a mess indoors.

Mum would *always* tell us how expensive shoes were and how we should look after them. If they were new, they had to be softened or 'worn in' before going out in them. If we came indoors with our shoes on, we'd be told off and… "God help you" if you damaged them at school or while playing out.

In a published book of poetry, I wrote in later years as an adult, one of the titles refers to this obsession Mum had, about looking after shoes to save money:

Goody Two Shoes

I've got a new pair of shoes
So, I've got to wear them in
Before I can wear them out
But Mum says I must never wear them in (doors)
And I definitely mustn't wear them out
I wish I'd bought a pair of plimsolls now

Anyway, we were on half-term holiday this particular

week, so I decided to clean the shoes on a Friday, as I would of course be helping Dad over the weekend.

When I went out into the garden to start, I couldn't find the shoes; they simply weren't there.

So, I came back in and asked Dad where he'd put them.

"In the usual place son – by the bin. You can't miss them."

"They're not there!"

After a few heated exchanges, it became apparent to Dad that indeed, they were not there. What became even more apparent, was the fact that the bin-men came on a Friday!

I have a lasting image of Dad running out of the house in stockinged feet, chasing after the bin-lorry wielding an 'adze'.

He returned four hours later in a terrible state; out of breath and triumphantly holding up one, yes one high-heeled shoe. I thought he was going to pass out through lack of oxygen. However, in bringing back only one shoe, he had made two fundamental errors; firstly, no one could wear it without the other and secondly, it only served to give Mum a weapon with which she could hit him... and she did!

When news got out about this unfortunate event, a friend of my Mother's – an ardent church-goer – approached her vicar for some help. He advised us all to attend church that Sunday and he would ask for a collection. We all attended (some more reluctant than others) in 'flip-flops.'

After the collection, the vicar said the church would keep half of it and gave Mum the rest. The residual amount, although gratefully received, would only be enough to buy half of us footwear, so three of us attended school for a week in flip-flops.

Dad was thankful, believe me, but a little disgruntled

about this fifty-fifty arrangement at his time of need (a need to appease Mum) and I recall him saying to the vicar:

"At least I didn't have to pay to get out of church this time!"

Back came the vicar's riposte: "I'm surprised you can remember!"

The pressure at school had been greatly reduced; the Local Authority and Governors were greatly relieved and appreciative. I was beginning to enjoy the role. Then Gwynneth and I suffered a traumatic experience with an unexpected miscarriage and I knew it was time for me to return home to the family's needs.

Chapter Seventeen

THE THIRD PINNACLE

I GOT shortlisted for a post in West Yorkshire. Downton Primary was again a three-form entry but larger than the Middle school in Oxford and more importantly, only an hour from home. So, I decided to drive up from my digs and have a look around, as well as glean some information from the staff and/or parents.

It was a good three-and-a-half-hour trip and consequently, by the time I got there was tired and in need of refreshment. The incumbent Head was brash, inhospitable and didn't even offer me a cup of tea, but the school looked clean, tidy (perhaps too tidy in my opinion) and far more welcoming than my previous two.

It was around October time that the interview was set for a January start. I was prepared for it and compared to my last, far more pleasant to be involved in. My latest successes were instrumental in my appointment, also the way I and the Governors 'clicked', but I think singing 'Kenny The Kangaroo' to the 'Reception' children was possibly the clincher.

Naturally, it fell to the Chair of Governors, a lady of advanced years, to inform me of their decision and she was magnificently northern over the phone:

"Well we've made our decision – do you want it or not?"

Leaving Donnington was a relief. It had been a hard eighteen months turning the school around. I was totally convinced that no future position could ever be as hard. For nine months we all lived at my small, terraced house, looking for a more suitable home. It was good to be a complete family once more and I was fully aware of how hard it had been for Gwynneth.

Mavis, a grand old lady, who lived a few doors down, was a wonderful neighbour. She was only knee high to a grasshopper but had the heart of a lion. She was the first person to welcome me to the house on the very day I moved in; offering me the traditional cup of sugar, milk and tea. She had been a welcome friend to us and a Fairy God-Mother-type to our children. She was sad when we moved to our new address in October 2001.

After two training days, and time to meet the staff, the children arrived in school.

In an effort to introduce myself to the Key Stage One and Two children, I decided to do a playground duty. As I was walking amongst the throngs, a young child came bounding up to me:

"Ey-oop Mr Franklin, I was laikin on t'yard an' someone stole m' snap."

For a moment, I thought he had a speech defect but when others chimed in with this foreign language I cried out for an interpreter. Luckily, a playground assistant did as her name suggests and translated for me. It would take me a long time to get my head around the local dialect and vernacular. Even when I started teaching English lessons and phonemes, I had concerned parents complaining that their children were putting the southern 'r' sound in words such as grass and castle. Anyone called Sandra, would laugh hysterically when I called them, repeating my soundings with an emphasised 'Sarrrndra'.

Incidentally, when my Son brought some high-school

friends home once, I was intrigued to know why they were all calling him 'Cavs'. When I enquired, one of them announced that it was because he sounded posh... "it's short for caviar".

To be fair, I felt completely out of my comfort zone, when I went down to visit the Foundation Stage children. For a start, little children stuck to my clothing like 'burdock burs'. It was a totally new experience for me and throughout my time there, I always admired the staff who looked after and taught the 0-5 years age range. In faith, I believed these groups to be the flagship of the school. Without doubt, these formative years are the most important and influential in a child's entire life. At this stage, children are like sponges, soaking up and assimilating all the basic life skills that they will later develop and apply to other learning processes.

Once, a parent asked me at what age should I start reading to my child. My response shocked her: "Whilst the child is still in the womb," was my reply, and I meant it!

Even at this stage in their early lives, children can distinguish between anger, happiness intonation and inflection. Musical sounds and words can be heard through the lining of the womb.

After the child is born, reading as a form of communication can start immediately. Reading pervades life and the earlier we can help children decode the written word, the greater their chances of reading with confidence and ultimately becoming more successful in their careers. The investment parents and teachers make in the first five years of a child's life, will ultimately determine their futures. I used to tell young parents they should greatly consider this piece of advice the next time they come home tired from work and plonk the children in front of the television because they can't be bothered to read to them. When children are at their most challenging, they need to be engaged and occupied in meaningful activities, especially after primary needs are satisfied.

On one of my early visits to the Nursery, I went down on my haunches to talk to a young girl, who perfectly illustrated the egocentric nature and literal understanding of this age:

"Hello, and what's your name?"

"My Dad's a milkman."

"Oh, that's interesting."

"What are you trying to do?"

"We are doing Maffs."

"I like Maths," – emphasising the correct pronunciation. "Tell me what you're doing."

"We have to add two and one."

"Do you know the answer?"

"No, not yet."

"Well, let me help you. If you have two balloons and I give you another balloon, how many balloons have you got altogether?"

She stared at me in a confused way and replied:

"We haven't done balloons yet!"

I truly believe supermarkets are amazing places to teach children, provided they are fed before being taken there.

After establishing myself at Downton, I made contact with the local Coop supermarket manager, who allowed me to bring small groups of children to be taught maths in the shop. What mathematical functions can't be taught in such a place? After the initial shop-lifting incidences, the whole arrangement was a roaring success:

Supermarkets

Supermarkets
Super places
For adults and children
To learn…
Colours
Reading
Writing
And Maths
Also on offer…
Weights
Shapes
Measures
Adding and subtraction
Special offers…
Division and multiplication
Super fruit
Super sizes
Buy one
Get one free
Sociology
Etiquette
'scuse me
After you
A wonderful
Enlightening environment
So why do so many parents
Take their kids there
To slap them!

In the early 'noughties', I was very much aware that the school desperately needed to open its doors to parents and invite them in to experience our teaching methodologies;

primarily as a means towards supporting their children at home. Many parents had not enjoyed their schooling and as a result, were either unwilling or unable to assist.

I had heard of a project down in Birmingham called I.N.S.P.I.R.E. which specifically sought to inspire reading education (hence the last three letters of the acronym).

I wanted to use this idea but expand it to involve other subjects, especially practical-based ones first, to gain the attention and interest of parents. The idea was to invite relatives into the first or last lesson of a chosen year-group to assist their child(ren). Fridays were chosen for the 'feel-good factor' and the timings meant that parents could come to school with their children before work, or arrive later in the afternoon for the lesson after work, before taking them home. There was more than one occasion when I personally had to or offered to approach managers or employers directly to allow workers time off for this idea. Indeed, one or two baulked at the notion, saying they had not been given time off for similar events, to which I replied:

"You should've been, children grow up too quickly."

I formulated a letter which stated that children could not take part in these workshops unless a relative attended. Some parents, not wishing to attend, thought this decision amounted to blackmail but changed their minds when I explained the terrible disappointment that some pupils felt when others' parents arrived for the lesson and theirs did not. In fact, all pupils took part and those without parents were sat with classroom assistants. The ruse worked!

I do not think it unfair to say, that I had a greater challenge trying to convince staff; some of whom did not want parents in school during teaching sessions. Indeed, some saw this as a threat, but I convinced them that it would drive up achievement and we could harness some of the adults' skills to help with our needs in school; not least of all, those of tradesmen or voluntary assistants.

I informed staff that I would not ask them to perform any task without my undertaking it first.

I asked them collectively to choose a practical-based subject, with which I could start the initiative. I could almost hear the machinations of their thought processes, trying to decide which would be the hardest subject for me to try and teach. It would not have mattered – they came up with Technology anyway. I took time to plan well; it had to succeed!

On the morning of the very first INSPIRE workshop, we had a ninety-nine per cent attendance and my Caretaker very kindly stayed to work with the unaccompanied pupil.

Each pair had an identically filled Chinese takeaway container, in which I had placed the following as well as A4 paper:

> A larger wooden disc
> A smaller wooden disc
> A longer wooden spindle
> A shorter wooden spindle
> Glue, paper-tabs, felt-tip pens
> Unnecessary 'blu-tack'
> Unnecessary sticky-tape
> Colouring pens/pencils

During the briefing, which was to be no longer than five minutes, I informed everyone that they were to make a gaming spinner which had to land on a number or colour and a championship spinner that had to spin for as long as possible. They had to make notes on their designs, recording what did and did not work.

The task was to last forty-five minutes, at the end of

which I would reveal some design recommendations such as the larger discs, set at a low centre of gravity on the longer spindle, should spin longer and the smaller discs with a higher centre of gravity on shorter spindles would fall over quicker.

The workshop was a hive of activity and both children and parents set about the task with a high degree of interest and eagerness. It was a pleasure watching them optimize their resources and bounce ideas off each other.

The outcome was remarkable! The winning competitive spinner was a small disc set halfway along the shorter spindle, which continued to spin for a considerable time. The winning gaming spinner was a larger disc, set on a higher centre of gravity using a longer spindle. More impressively, the latter would land on the number four each time it was spun! This was achieved with the use of the *unnecessary* resources and probably said more about my caretaker's betting skills, than the surprising outcome of his gaming spinner!

The lesson was hugely successful and very well received by all.

That following Monday, I collected in all the follow-up work that I requested:

Each piece of work explained the task, listed the materials used, illustrated the spinners and gave a conclusion of the outcome. It is true that much of the written follow-up work revealed evidence of significant parental involvement, as pointed out by some staff. However, I mitigated this by submitting that the parents were there and their job was indeed to work with and support the child…mission accomplished!

The resulting displays were fabulous and there was a tangible feeling of pride in a charged atmosphere when parents came back to view them. Moreover, many asked when the next one was to take place.

Eventually, all staff came on board with the idea and the workshops became increasingly competitive.

The astonishing feature of this initiative was that it went on for longer than ten years and the parental attendance was always incredibly high; rarely falling below ninety-eight per cent.

The project developed into adult learning classes, on-site and within the school day, resulting in continual adult displays to inspire the children.

When Ofsted visited, I delivered an art workshop INSPIRE session for two classes and their families in the hall, based around the design of 'Gaudi Chimneys' using clay. Ofsted were impressed and gave our 'Community' based work an excellent grading.

It is a point of pride, that a significant number of those attending parents went on to become voluntary or salaried assistants and two became teachers. Voluntary workers were always encouraged as a form of recruitment drive for future full or part-time staff. They had the chance to see if our school was right for them and vice versa.

My strapline was: "PARENTS form the greater part of PARTNERSHIP" (seven out of the eleven letters to be precise)

To this very day, I should consider this initiative outside of teaching itself, to be my most successful.

In other ways of raising the profile of the school, I managed to get celebrities to come and present whole school assemblies and workshops. Among these were Don Lind, a 1985 Orbiter Challenger astronaut and Jeff Rich, the Status Quo rock group drummer.

As well as providing engaging and participational workshops, these guests also attracted national, regional, local television and radio.

Chapter Eighteen

ROPING UP –
A MULTINATIONAL TEAM

IN FEBRUARY of 2002, the Local Authority invited twelve Headteachers to visit South Africa, on an exchange visit to Gauteng Province to make positive links with their schools. This was to be followed up with a reciprocal visit the next year, with the dozen representatives and their schools playing hosts.

Gauteng is one of South Africa's nine provinces. Its name in Sotho-Tswana means 'place of gold.'

It was too good an opportunity to miss, as I dearly wanted our school to be making an embedded impact on the international scene before our next inspection. We had hit the right bells so-to-speak, on the local and national requirements.

It was a twelve-hour connection flight that was quite uncomfortable in economy class, as I couldn't unfurl my legs, which meant a lot of stretching and walking around the voluminous cabin. As mentioned previously, I'm not a natural aviator, but luckily these long-distant flights are often made above the weather and unwelcome turbulence.

When we all eventually arrived in the oppressive heat of a Johannesburg terminal, we were teamed up with our host Headteachers. I was paired with a rather regal, unflappable Black Headteacher with a noble presence, called Floyd Malinga.

Suffering from fatigue, the plan after our initial meeting, was to rest up for the day and begin an exhausting itinerary the following day, commencing with a visit to our respective schools.

Floyd drove me back to his new, rather modest dwelling, which was part of a re-housing scheme to drive down – as it were – the number of 'shanty-towns' in the district.

He lived there with his wife, whilst his son lived with his Mother, a Sangoma or healing priestess.

Because of its global position, the sun sinks rapidly in South Africa and darkness soon comes. This must have had an influence on my body clock, so I went to my room to sleep.

As I was unpacking, there was a loud bang outside the window, which sounded very much like a gunshot. I rather panicked and ran out of my bedroom, into the small adjacent lounge where Floyd was sitting with his wife and cried:

"Floyd, I think I've just heard a gunshot from outside my window."

In a calm, unemotional, expressionless but reassuring way, he replied:

"Yeeees, some kids probably playing with a gun."

"Playing with a gun!" I thought: "Where have I come to?"

"Yeeees, you'll be alright, they'll soon go away."

And they did, but I didn't get much sleep that night. Then Floyd woke me at 'early-o-clock'.

I sat down at the table and Floyd's wife brought me a bowl of 'pap' or corn porridge:

"We have a very busy day today Paul. Many people

want to meet you, so we won't be home until late tonight. School starts at 8 o-clock, so we must be on our way.

The sun had already risen into the cobalt blue-silken backdrop of an unblemished sky, as we entered the dust-encrusted car on Floyd's drive. Even at that time in the morning, wildlife was sheltering from the relentless morning heat and small dust devils sprung up along the roadside on our short journey.

On the way to school, we discussed the activities of the night before and Floyd settled my troubled mind, by saying he was politically active in the area and I would be safe if I kept with him. I explained ironically, that in our country, that might put me more at risk. The joke wasn't lost on him, in fact he spoke very good English; probably his weakest after eight other languages, including tribal tongues and Afrikaans. Nevertheless, all through my stay, I never felt intimidated in an area that had a high crime rate whilst I was in his company, even though I certainly attracted a lot of attention.

On arrival at the school, I was warmly greeted by Floyd's senior staff; both his wonderful Deputy Heads called Bophelo and Nico, Heads of Year and Chair of Governors.

Staff and children performed dances and sang cultural songs, in a welcoming display of music, colour and exuberance; reserved only I thought, for royalty.

After the celebrations ended, I could hear staff and children calling out "Pule," "Pule."

I asked Floyd how they knew my name. He suddenly laughed and said:

"They're not saying Paul; they're happily calling you 'The bringer of rain' and that hasn't happened for a long time. You've brought your English weather with you."

Sure enough, it had started to drizzle and this in itself

generated great excitement throughout the whole school. Teasingly, Floyd said:

"They think you are the rain God."

Once again, I replied ironically:

"My association with this at home would also put me at risk."

Floyd was Head of a combined Primary and Secondary school, called Ebony Park, with well over two-thousand pupils and just *two* toilets. The out-buildings were in a dilapidated state and only a few were covered with corrugated iron roofs. It was dusty and dirty, with average-sized classes of sixty-plus children of differing ages.

That morning, two other sights beyond that of my welcome, have remained as vivid memory-moments to this day:

I saw many young children, no older than seven years, arrive after walking the same distance as their age in kilometres. Upon arrival at the threshold of their classrooms, they would produce a small round brush and dust off the accumulated sand and dirt on their clothes from the journey. They then entered their crowded teaching space, with a small jotter and 'betting'-sized pencil.

As the rain got progressively heavier, children would take old bin liners from their pockets, which had head- and armholes cut out and cover themselves.

It was humbling and heart-rending to witness and I unashamedly shed a tear; it wouldn't be the last.

It became abundantly clear to me, after talking to so many children and Floyd, that school was regarded by all as a privilege rather than a right, as well as a place of sanctity and security. The level of abuse at home for too many of these children was disturbing. The attendance rate for a school of this size, was staggeringly high, for the above reasons.

Oh boy, did I make a point of telling everyone about

this, when I got back to school with the photographic evidence!

We were hovering around ninety-three-to-four per cent attendance, with a target of ninety-five and a pupil count of less than a quarter of Floyd's school. To achieve this target, I engaged the help of local industry to fund prizes every half-term for children who achieved a one-hundred per cent attendance. It wasn't unusual for a boy and girl to take home a cycle each, after winning the '100 Grand Draw'. With these types of incentive, children began to pressurize their parents into getting them to school, even if they didn't feel well.

Floyd neither had the finances nor the need to engage in such a project of encouragement; to be able to leave their homes and (in many cases) walk *vast* distances to school to learn, was enough incentive. Again, this was another notable case of child resilience, that still to this day, occupies my mind and for me justifies 'Third World' relief aid.

After a busy day, Floyd said that after going home to change, there was a long line of people wanting to see me, starting with his sister.

I never saw Floyd off his mobile phone; a familiar sight that has pervaded my long association with him. I've often remarked that he should have it surgically removed.

To be fair, I was tired and in need of sustenance before we arrived at Floyd's sister's house. After the initial greetings, she enquired as to whether I was hungry and returned with a local delicacy – a plate of *chicken's feet*:

"Oh, that's unusual, you have a different custom to us at home. We normally throw the chicken's feet away and eat the chicken. You appear to do it the other way around."

The flippant remark had hardly left my lips when a wave of guilt attacked me, thinking I just might have insulted the entire family, who may not have been able to afford chicken.

She smiled and said I should eat them all, as it would be considered an insult if I didn't.

I momentarily surveyed the victuals and then without hesitation, trying to hide my inner disdain, set about eating the first. They were quite hard to negotiate. I tried sucking the gelatinous flesh from the bone and when that didn't work, set about chewing the skin of rubber-band-like consistency. The claws, occasionally, pricked my lips. I tried not to expose my abhorrence throughout the ordeal but, clearly, my revulsion was apparent by the time I got to my eighth fowl foot.

"You look as if you've eaten enough," said Floyd's sister.

"Aren't you having any?" I replied, feeling subjected to examination and criticism.

"Don't be ridiculous, we never eat them, they taste like shit!"

She and Floyd howled with laughter, as the realization of what had just taken place struck me. I'd been 'stitched up' like the proverbial kipper'. It was minutes before the mirth had subsided and I felt not a little embarrassed.

"Would you like some chicken and sandwiches now?" she sympathetically inquired

"She is a joker," said Floyd.

After a little while and some pleasant conversation, Floyd was ushering me to the next engagement. We were to go to the houses of both his Deputies, his Chair of Governors, his Mother and a representative from the Gauteng Local Authority. All had laid on a sizeable spread and, in turn, had invited numerous guests to join us. There was much handshaking, conversation and inescapable eating, so as not to offend people's preparations and hospitality.

By the end of the event-filled evening, I was tired and suffering acute discomfort, from the over-indulgence. As I struggled to re-enter Floyd's car, I couldn't help but recall those hilarious scenes in a Christmas episode of *The Vicar of Dibley* when the title character tries to fulfil her obligations by attempting to eat three meals; as well as entering into a Brussel sprout-eating competition.

When we arrived home, I waddled like a duck up the path to Floyd's front door, praying for some respite in the bullet-disturbed silence of my temporary bedroom.

As we entered the front door, Floyd's kind wife had not only prepared a surprise meal but had waited for our return before eating anything. She commented on how late we were and Floyd apologised profusely.

Whilst she was out of the room collecting the hot food from the oven, Floyd buttonholed me:

"I'm sorry, Pule, try to eat something, she's made an effort."

Nodding my head, as if I had just agreed to embark upon a suicidal mission behind enemy lines, I sat down to await a captured prisoner's torture session.

She had prepared chicken and other 'treats' which must have cost them a small fortune and threw down an appetite-abating portion of pap!

Events had got seriously discomforting now, as I tried to force unrequired food into my mouth.

Now it felt like the climax to a 'Man versus Food programme, where the food-combatant masochist, is struggling against the clock to consume the final mouthfuls of cholesterol-filled clagginess.

I desperately needed a drink and Floyd obliged me with a bottle of orange Tango. I took a deep gulp and sat back. Suddenly, memories of my ordeal with a sachet of Resolve flashed into my head, as my internal organs detonated! This prompted, nay, demanded a requisite and immediate evacuation of my bowels. To my hosts' bewilderment, I rushed to the toilet feet away, barely managing to close the door (for what benefit it offered) just in time for the deluge, accompanied by an explosive blast that would have easily registered 6.9 on the Richter Scale. The tiny 'House on the Prairie' palpably shook, so deafness alone, wouldn't have disguised my embarrassing plight. The noise was like the doppler effect of a passing juggernaut, sounding its air horns continuously!

Twenty minutes later I returned to the table and confused looks on the faces of my hosts, bathed in sweat but revelling in the welcome relief.

Back in the day, I carried with me an Olympus OM1, thirty-five-millimetre camera, that I'd purchased over twenty-five years before in Riyadh. It wasn't because I purposely wanted to impede my developmental and tech-nological capabilities, but rather because it took better images than my mobile phone at the time.

I was snapping away quicker than a *Vogue Magazine* model photographer; building up a comprehensive library of pictures to accompany my diary entries. Naturally, I ran out of film so Floyd kindly drove me to a shopping mall in Midrand after school.

Midrand is predominantly a white South-African town, that black people wouldn't have been able to enter during Apartheid – a word meaning apartness in Afrikaans. The difference in style and accommodation was instantly apparent.

I decided to window-shop for a while, looking for gifts that I would inevitably give to my hosts before leaving. Whilst browsing, I was acutely aware of white shoppers giving me contemptuous glares. At first, I didn't give the scornful looks much consideration, but after a while, when the reason for them became clear. I started returning the stares, without breaking eye contact until the onlookers had passed.

Floyd glanced at his watch and suggested we got a move on to buy film, as the shops were due to close. As we approached a chemist, Floyd offered to go and purchase what I needed, which gave me a few more minutes to browse. As he approached the glass door, the shopkeeper saw him and turned the 'open' sign around. Floyd turned on his heels and headed back towards me, unaware that I had just witnessed his wrongful dismissal. I glanced at my watch and saw there was easily enough time to make a purchase. I questioned Floyd about the incident, but he merely said the shop had closed, clearly embarrassed but not surprised by the racist act. I was at once incensed and strode off to the shop, in spite of Floyd's protestations. As *I* approached the shop door, as if to justify my anger, the shopkeeper turned the sign back and let me in!

"Why did you close the door in my friend's face?" I demanded to know.

The man tried to usher me back to the entrance, but I wouldn't budge.

"He came to buy some film for me, but I wouldn't purchase anything from you, even if you were the only outlet in South Africa. It's 2002, not 1952. Would you not serve Nelson Mandela?!"

I stormed out of the building and deliberately put my arm around Floyd's shoulder in a gesture of defiance, not only for the benefit of the shopkeeper but any other reprehensible individual with similar inclinations. This was not to be the only case of racist abuse, that I would witness.

In faith, Apartheid is over *de jure*, but still to this day exists *de facto*!

This disgraceful incident was going to be the powerfully delivered subject matter of assemblies I led, when I got back and not just in my school...

Although the twelve visiting Headteachers rarely got together, because of the time commitments of their individual itineraries, it was arranged that we would all, along with our hosts, travel to Mpumalanga and the Kruger National Park; an exciting prospect that generated much anticipation.

On the morning of our early departure, we all convened at the main building of the Local Authority, where there was a rather tired-looking minibus and driver for that matter, waiting for us. Floyd was in full conversational flow with his conjoined mobile phone, so I struck up a conversation with a 'Coloured' Headteacher, who possessed a fabulous and aristocratic-sounding Dutch name: Don Van Der Westhuizen. Don was a secondary school Headteacher of well-built proportions, who clearly looked as if he had played contact sport at a good level. He had a quiet disposition but nevertheless, exuded an air of confidence, dominance and responsibility with a protective nature. I wanted to get to know this man and in the course of doing so, was to strike up a lasting friendship, that we still share to this day. Don has become one of my closest friends, whom you could count on the fingers of an Arab thief's hand!

We all squeezed ourselves into the confined space of the minibus and headed north-east, on a journey that would take us around eight hours to complete. The atmosphere was dynamic and high-spirited.

Leaving the 'City of Gold' on a single-track road, we were greeted with a view of extraordinary contrasts. Palatial-looking premises gave way to more modest housing, which in turn revealed the rather gloomy, unappealing and shanty-looking outlying areas of Johannesburg. Soon we were driving through the sun-drenched, burnt sienna brown canvas of the veld (meaning field in Afrikaans) that is used mainly for pasture and farmland.

After several stops to refuel, restock, refresh and relieve ourselves, we eventually approached Mpumalanga; the second-smallest province in South Africa after Gauteng.

The landscape took on an altogether different appearance from our earlier sightings from the vehicle. Here was lush green vegetation and a stifling level of humidity, that left everyone bathing in sweat.

Looking from the vehicle, we could see many poor native people who were 'clawing' a living out of fashioning animals from deadwood using basic tools.

They looked desperately under-nourished and shoddily dressed. I asked our hosts if we could stop and look at the 'road-art'.

As we perused the wares, an overwhelming wave of sadness and admiration enveloped me; I wanted to support the endeavours of these people-whose talents were driven by circumstances and necessity – by purchasing some of their beautiful wooden sculptures.

One chap I noticed, was carving a large antelope from a single piece of wood. He said it was a Kudu, but he hadn't finished it yet. Don took hold of it, asking him for his knife and started to shave small slithers of wood from its hide. He then handed them back to the passive artist. I said I'd like to buy it when it was completed but could he keep hold of it for a day or so. To this he agreed and asked me to promise to come back. I did so and the man continued to work on it as we left.

Our group purchased pieces from other vendors and were amazed at how beautifully carved they were for such low prices. At the time, there were seventeen rand to the pound and some of these carvings were under ten rand. Back home a trendy studio would be selling these for between twenty and forty pounds at least.

It is perhaps interesting to note at this stage, that one of our group contacted us all when she got back, to say that she had a woodworm infestation from one of the items she brought home. This prompted us all to have our souvenirs treated. Nevertheless, my home is still adorned with these beautiful artworks. My most prized possessions are a tiny bird made from wood, string and real feathers, that collapses when you push upwards on the base; whilst re-erecting itself when released and a small Christmas tree made from a beer can. Both articles cost less than a pound each. However, the craftsmanship is exquisite and I'll always treasure them.

As we travelled to our hotel, the roads outside the Kruger were full of people trying to sell their art or begging. Some areas were rife with disease and we had all been advised to get immunization against hepatitis A and B, typhoid, meningitis, tetanus and, perhaps more importantly, malaria.

We all had a reasonably early night as we were going into the National Park at five-o-clock the next morning. This was considered the best time to see animals feeding before they sheltered from the heat of the midday sun.

The Kruger National Park is just under 20,000 square kilometres in size and only slightly smaller than Belgium. It is home to one-hundred and forty-seven mammal species, one-hundred-and-fourteen types of reptile, over five-hundred bird species and more than 2,000 flora. Tourists hope to spot the animals known as 'The Big Five' – lion, elephant, rhino, leopard and buffalo.

The decision to enter the park using our own minibus was taken by the Local Authority host to save costs. On reflection, we should have been far happier paying for guides and a safer safari bus; even these do not guarantee personal safety.

Within minutes of entering the Park, our driver slowed up on the track, to allow what can only be described as a large, hairy caterpillar the size of a cucumber to pass. To our left one of the headteachers spotted an elephant calf, munching on a shrub not too far from the vehicle. Against the backdrop of 'aahhs', 'oohs' and frenetic camera-clicking, came an almighty scream:

"There's a bull elephant charging towards us!"

"Put your bloody foot down!" cried Don.

He did, but accidentally slipped the transmission into a higher gear. The van crept forward in a laboured fashion. The monster caterpillar seemed to be making more ground.

The L.A. official quickly leaned towards our chauffeur and *slapped* his face, to which the driver seemed to respond by banging the gearstick into 'first', lurching the minibus quickly forward in a howl of high revolutions. As the bull gradually lost momentum and returned to its calf, there was an audible sound of relief and expletives shared amongst us.

Even now I get flashbacks of this moment and recall just how close that huge, handsome beast got to us, whilst obviously defending its youngster.

As we moved on, I just caught sight of a large bird of prey plummet out of the sky and disappear behind a large bush. It re-emerged moments later with a writhing snake in its talons.

"Christ," I thought. We really had entered our very own 'killing fields'. Our surroundings were so wild, natural, beautiful and brutal, but nature has its own unique way of establishing an equilibrium of existence. In contrast, of course, mankind (or rather unkind) has its own way of disrupting or destroying the circle of life.

In 2017, sixty-seven elephants were poached in the Kruger National Park, but even more disturbing is the fact that five-hundred-and-four rhinos were poached. With the help of modern technology, these numbers are decreasing, but although elephant numbers are slowly recovering, recent reports from 'SANParks' reveal there are only 3,529 white rhinos and 268 black rhinos left. Most of the horns from the latter end up in Vietnam or China, which begs the question: – why cannot these unscrupulous and immoral recipients just bite their fingernails, where the same protein, keratin is found, or be forced to watch *Springwatch* on a loop from their cells, to discover the beauty of living creatures.

It is not just poaching that is the problem. Wildfires do spring up occasionally, causing extensive damage. However, in 2007 a middle-aged man was arrested for *starting* a fire in the Kruger near the Phabeni Entrance, but only after he had set three others going along the road between the gate and Skukuza rest camp. The fires were started at midday and were still blazing at 4 o'clock. I know because I was there with my family and Don's. It was heart-breaking to watch animals, including a black rhino, walk amongst the debris trying to find food.

Now, we spent some hours in the minibus trying to spot more of the 'Big Five' from a safer distance and pulled up at a place in the open savanna to observe some buffalo in the distance.

As somebody opened the sliding door, for us to take photographs, Floyd noticed a dozing lioness, directly alongside our parked vehicle in the long grass. She was of no immediate threat to us nor clearly the buffalo; having already eaten or just taking respite from the intolerable heat. Even so, this was an even closer encounter of the killing kind!

We were lucky to spot three of the five, but come mid-afternoon, there was little chance of seeing any more in the suffocating heat, so we headed for one of the rest camps and then back to our hotel.

The following morning our group were driven to a place called 'God's Window', a beautiful vantage point on the Drakensberg escarpment, overlooking the Blyde River Nature Reserve.

Looking out from this position, it becomes immediately obvious how it got its name. The views are spectacular, with beautiful towering rock formations, cascading waterfalls of immense power, canyons and lush forested ravines. One can see the open veld, hills and trees disappear into the horizon. It is as I say, a memory-moment never to be forgotten.

After a while, the L.A. host suggested we made our way back to Ebony Park in Johannesburg. It took some time and much persuasion, to get him to agree to return to the street artist I had promised to buy the kudu from. I was not prepared to renege on my promise and so reluctantly, he ordered the driver to drive the short distance to the sculptor.

Upon our arrival, the craftsman immediately recognised me as I alighted from the van and made a beeline for me with the sculpture.

"How much?" I enquired.

"Thirty–five rand," came the reply.

"Too much," said the L.A. host.

"What?" I proclaimed.

Then a fierce discussion took place between our man and the artist, which left me feeling very embarrassed.

"That's only a little over two pounds I declared".

"Still too much," said our host and in a battle of exchanges wore the vendor down to fifteen rand.

"OK, and an apple," said the artist; at which point I froze with pity.

I went back to the van and, gathering a small bag of apples, gave them to him. He immediately took one and before our eyes devoured it in an instant!

"He's starving," I said and with an overpowering sense

161

of guilt and anger, slammed fifty rand into his hand and encouraged others in our group to buy more pieces of art.

The L.A. host said we could upset their economy with our generosity. I was incensed!

"This man is desperate for food and he's got a skill that would earn him thousands of rand in the UK".

"Sadly, this is not the UK," he replied.

"Sadly, for him, you're right," came the riposte, as I went to my case and got out some clothes which I gladly handed to the over-appreciative recipient.

Judging, by the amount of street art I had purchased, I was going to have to leave more clothing behind, in order to get it all back home.

I warmly shook the dishevelled person's hand and at once felt that I had achieved some good. At the very least, I had proved to him that some people are worth their word. His lingering wave and less-vexed countenance made for a memory-moment I should never forget.

I once purchased an African soap-stone candlestick from an art studio in Leeds for just five pounds. How small a payment must the producer of this piece have received?

Within an hour of our journey back, I glanced in the driver's rear-view mirror from the back of the van, to see that he was showing signs of fatigue. His eyelids were flickering and his head was nodding. No one else had noticed, so I brought it to the attention of Don. By now we were on the main road and darkness had descended. Don caught a glimpse of his tiredness and spoke to the L.A. host in Afrikaans. He too saw the driver succumbing to exhaustion and without a moment's hesitation leaned forward and *slapped* the driver *again*! If this had been a circus clown act, I have no hesitation in thinking it would have been amusing, but there are other less violent and more acceptable rules of social engagement.

I said to Don that no amount of slapping was going to cure his weariness, so he and I shared the driving of the minibus back, over a gruelling time period of eight hours, whilst the driver gratefully slept in the back.

When we eventually got back, everyone was close to collapse, but we all agreed it had been an incredible experience. Moreover, Don and I had cemented a life-long friendship.

I had the opportunity to teach at Don's secondary school for a day and used a 'Big Book' of poems, that I had borrowed from Key-Stage one at home.

We had enormous fun putting the text to a 'Rap-rhythm' in a class of eighteen-year-olds!

That night, I went out for drinks with Don and his associates and again made life-long friendships. I could not stay at his house that night, because he already had a guest, but he took me to the house of a friend called Cycil who was a university lecturer. He and his wife Sherry were very, very kind and hospitable. I tell you; the generosity of these people knew no bounds.

Our time in South Africa passed too quickly, but there was much to be gleaned from our stay and more importantly, to share with our staff and pupils.

Many of the cultural exhibits brought back, formed a semi-permanent display for our central area. Other treasured possessions, such as slides and reading matter were priceless content for our programmes of study across subject areas. Whole-school assemblies benefited hugely from the primary source of evidence.

Chapter Nineteen

DEATH ON THE PEAK

IT WAS back to work after the February half-term and it was my intention to improve the technology within the school.

About this time the Government were dishing out a limited number of laptops to schoolteachers in a push to promote computer literacy and 'Smartboard' teaching.

It is perhaps understandable that some older members of staff resisted, or reluctantly adopted the modern approaches to teaching and learning; entering the twenty-first century, protesting and clutching on to the past methods of pedagogy that were tried and trusted.

By the same token, I've always rejected the phrase 'to reach or fulfil one's potential' because if one believes in lifelong learning then by definition, it's not achievable.

At first, one or two smartboards found their way onto the premises, with the youngsters rubbing their hands with glee. It was clear we needed more for a three-form entry school such as ours and I wanted to introduce them early into our flagship Foundation Stage. However, the Local Authority were adamant that no departments within the budget, other than 'technology' could be used to purchase more.

Early models were placed on trolleys to allow teachers to share the resource, but others were available to be screwed to the wall for static teaching.

I came up with the idea that if they were permanently fixed to the wall, then we might regard them as fixtures and fittings and therefore plunder the furnishing and fixtures budget. We were not in dire need of new cupboards or shelving, so I approached our legal department for advice on how these semantics might work in our favour. They confirmed that I was able to interpret the language in this way without the authority having recourse against my decision. In view of this, I bought six more despite the overtures of disagreement from higher authority.

I have always maintained as a Head that rules, rather than laws are for guidance and are open to interpretation, but it should not be a battle for us or the children.

Our school was going to be at the vanguard of change and once the hardware arrived, I set about letting the media, parents and other colleagues know.

A major push on teacher training ensued and it was not long before each Year Centre had technology for the age.

A flurry of laptops later and a majority of staff were accessing a wealth of information and computer-generated images at their fingertips.

There was a buzz about the place when we closed for Easter and everyone was happy at the prospects of the forthcoming summer term.

I received an unexpected call from Ken with some wretched news during the break. Geraldine had contracted terminal cancer and was in the final stages of the disease.

Ken intimated that it was her wish to see me before the end and could I get down to them as soon as possible. It was a race against time. I told him I'd leave immediately.

I thought it a brave decision on her part, because,

unlike Kay, she was aware and cared nothing about the shock she might present to her visitors. I remember her as a bubbly, fun-loving Irish blond with more than a modicum of impishness. She had made the right call and knew those who loved her, would understand her beauty still lay within a body that had failed her.

I stayed overnight in a hotel near Wheathampstead and prepared for my visit the next morning.

I arrived about nine-thirty the following morning and the nurse was still with her.

"Don't mind me, I'm just having a bed-bath," were her first words to me.

"Why don't you use the bath upstairs like everybody else?"

She giggled and I still recognized my childhood friend beneath the frightful effects of the rampant malignancy. She was incredibly thin and looked as if I might pick her up with one hand.

I caught sight of what appeared to be a pack of Chinese crackers:

"These are no good for you, not enough calories. I should have brought some Yorkshire puds."

She giggled again and highlighted my incorrigible behaviour.

We reminisced about many events from childhood school, to Saudi and teaching. There was so much to smile about and all the time I fought back the emotion to cry.

Just as I was about to leave, she asked if I could come back the next day:

"I thought you'd never ask!"

I kissed her and left.

The next morning, on my way to see her, I passed a greengrocer's shop and popped in to buy a single yellow capsicum pepper. I asked the shopkeeper to place it in a brown paper bag.

When I arrived at Geraldine's house, I was surprised to see so many visitors around her bed.

"Hi Geraldine, have you invited them all along to see your next bed-bath"?

A ripple of laughter broke out:

"I've bought a present for you."

This was met with confused faces.

"Why have you gone to the bother?"

"It's no bother, open it."

She pulled out the content and looked at me with a confused expression, as did the group around her.

"Why have you got me a pepper?"

"Because I thought it matched the colour of your skin beautifully."

I detected a sharp intake of breath and a sense of incredulity from the people around the bed; their eyes transfixed on me, with mouths wide open in astonishment. My eyes however were trained on Geraldine's. A wry grin appeared on her face and then her shoulders started to move up and down as she was consumed with laughter. It was infectious and her reaction was the permission for everyone else to release their tension. Soon the room was filled with laughter and those beautiful, youthful blue eyes shone so brightly, as tears of mirth flowed.

It was a long and sad journey back and I cried a great deal; mainly from witnessing the strength and dignity with which this brave woman faced her inevitable demise.

Ken called me about three days later to tell me she had passed away peacefully. He then inquisitively asked me what I had said to her to make her so happy.

"She shone like a bright light for the last few days," he said.

Chapter Twenty

SNOW SQUALL

MY BROTHER-IN-LAW had a great idea for us all to rent a minibus and drive to the Austrian resort of Zell am See during the Christmas and New Year of 2002/3, for a skiing holiday. I had never skied in my life and here I was at the age of forty, agreeing to the preposterous idea of driving all the way to the mountains to be taught by him!

After an interminable journey to Salzburg, we eventually arrived at our lodgings and collected our rented skiwear. Dressed like an accomplished downhill competitor, but feeling the anxiety levels and grave misgivings of the complete novice that I was, we humped our equipment in leaden boots to the cable car. Upon our arrival at the top, Julian, Claire and Gwynneth (who could ski) decided it would be a good idea to take themselves off to reconnoitre the local area without a map and leave me and my parents with the kids. I thought they would return in a short while, but they never came back!

After a prolonged period of waiting, I decided to call upon the services of Mum and Dad to look after the youngsters, whilst I attempted to self-teach myself, by stumbling up the end of a ski run. Having no idea how to stop on skis, I recklessly clicked myself into them and pointed myself downhill. They're very slippery. Even on this lower incline, I shot off like a bullet and only succeeded in stopping myself, by falling over; thus breaking my thumb into the bargain!

I wearily limped back to where the kids were being looked after and decided it would be better to spend some time with them. Harry was four at the time. He came to greet me and then for some reason, unexpectedly ran off. I tried as hard as I might to catch up with him, lumbering along in my Frankenstein's monster-like boots, but inevitably lost him in the thronging crowd. In an instant, he was gone! In a few moments, fear and alarm racked my mind. I started to cry his name out at the top of my voice. People just looked back at me with indifference. I struggled to run back to my parents in my ridiculous unwieldy and cumbersome footwear and in my panicking state, asked them to search bars and restaurants, whilst I went further afield. Anyone who has lost a child, even for moments, knows only too well the net of dark foreboding, fright and terror that descends. I lost him for a full fifteen minutes! The horror went on for what seemed an intolerable length of time. Worryingly, it was getting dark and people were dispersing and travelling back down the mountain. I hollered and accosted skiers in all directions, not caring that my shouting might set off an avalanche. Eventually, bathed in sweat and sinking to my knees in tears, I was approached by a Dutchman with Harry in tow. He was as blond as my son and looked to be more like his father. I could have hugged him – the Dutchman I mean. He told me that he had been queueing for the cable car when he spotted Harry lining up beside him.

"Are you Harry?" he enquired above the noise of the mechanism and my shouts for help. "Yes, I'm trying to find my mummy, she's gone missing." *She's* gone missing?!

Thanking the man repeatedly and profusely (I think it warranted a hug), I returned to the rest of the worried party and we eventually made our way back, not knowing what had happened to the other three. We were later to find out that they had got lost trying to make their way back to us and had to catch a bus from the other side of the mountain. Despite my accusatory response to their apologies, I couldn't help but feel grateful that we were all together again and that my prodigal wife had been oblivious and indeed not exposed to the worry and suffering that we had all endured.

Whenever I hear the track 'Bring him home' from *Les Miserables*, I'm transported back to that event.

One thing that I did learn from this experience, was that I really did want to ski and in February 2004 we flew the four hours to Bulgaria to receive lessons.

When we arrived at the airport for our departure, I casually asked at the Monarch check-in desk, what type of aircraft we would be flying in. The assistant laughed out loud, saying that it wouldn't be a British company aircraft, but rather an old, clapped-out, Russian-built Tupolev,

In his words: "One right out of *Austin Powers*' own personal fleet." He found this comment highly amusing as he watched my disturbed countenance and followed it up with:

"Wait 'til you see its livery."

As we walked up to the tired, old, 1970s-built aircraft, waiting on the tarmac apron we could see that it had been painted in all colours of the rainbow, including pink stripes.

The interior was worn and threadbare and the food offered comprised a dried-up salami sandwich, followed by a Mars bar for dessert.

After arriving at our hotel, where I ripped my trousers on a nail sticking out of the bedframe. we met a wonderfully accomplished skier called Maria, an ex-Olympian downhiller, who enabled us to become adept parallel skiers within a week. Harry was then left in ski-school and in subsequent years, French-speaking ski-schools, which he was unhappy about, but which were excellent in bringing him to a high standard. After his escapade in Austria, we put a full harness on him, like a guide dog. I didn't intend to take it off him until he was at upper school.

After a successful week of skiing, the moment came that I had been most dreading – the journey back. At Plovdiv airport, we took off in pouring rain and when we eventually got back to Manchester, the aircraft was 'stacked' for thirty minutes. Each time we circled round the airport, the engines were boosted to a howling crescendo and screamed as if they were breaking up under the strain.

After landing, I hugged each of the cabin staff. I knew they had to go back up again!

Chapter Twenty-One

TURNAROUND

LATE INTO the summer term of 2003, the South Africans made their reciprocal visit and were hosted by the Headteachers they had accommodated. Naturally, Floyd stayed with my family, but it was equally good to see the others again, especially Don. We collected our guests from a welcoming function at the Local Authority's main training facility, set in its beautiful grounds.

The South African party looked resplendent in their traditional costumes, especially the women dressed in stunning hats and dresses of primary colours. The one striking feature I have noted about travelling Africans is how much dignity they reveal about themselves, in the clothes they wear.

After much merriment, chit-chat and refreshments, we took our respective Headteachers home.

It took me about forty minutes to get back and then introduced Floyd to the family. Laura was around eleven years old at the time and Harry (addressed by Floyd as 'Muscle-man') was four. Harry was kicking a ball about and Floyd joined in, showing some remarkable talent.

We had a drink and then Gwynneth suggested I take Floyd to his room. When he entered, he expressed palpable concern about the windows not having security bars.

"Don't worry Floyd, you're unlikely to hear any

gunshots this evening and if you do, it'll only be some blokes shooting at clay-pigeons... not each other! He smiled wryly at me and looked at his watch bewilderingly.

"It's 10 o'clock and still light!"

"The wonders of British Summer Time," I declared. "Goodnight!"

The drive to school and back was an hour each way, but it gave me adequate time to talk to Floyd who meticulously recorded just about everything I said, or he saw. Being a local politician as well as a Headteacher, he had a wealth of questions to ask; primarily statistical, such as, how many pupils we had in the school, their funding per capita and so on. The man had a data-brain.

Floyd made a huge impact upon his arrival with the staff and pupils alike, virtually becoming a celebrity within the community. He was both kind and reverential when speaking to people of any age and his addresses to the school in assemblies were captivating; all characteristics of a great educator.

The itinerary here was as busy as in South Africa and after a few days in school, it was decided to take the visitors to York. The Local Authority had organised a coach, which meant transportation for all of us was so much easier, as well as keeping the group together.

We all arranged to meet at my school as the car park was big enough for all our individual cars and the coach. The South Africans turned up in their impressive outfits and looked magnificent.

After sightseeing for some time, one of the party asked if we could visit 'Betty's' tea shop. I suspected it would be terribly busy and was not surprised to see a queue the entire way around the building.

"Looks like we won't get in, Paulus," said Don in his low mellifluous voice.

"I'll see what I can do."

I entered the building and politely asked if I could see the manager. Within minutes he arrived on the top floor where I was waiting.

"How can I be of help sir?" he asked.

This was going to take some balls!

"Outside, I have Chief Malinga of the Sotho tribe with his three wives (there were three women Headteachers) and entourage. He has a busy itinerary and will be leaving York very soon but has expressed a wish to stop and refresh himself at the internationally renowned 'Betty's' tea shop. Would there be any possibility of accommodating him?"

The manager was 'jump-started' to give a flurry of orders and directions towards several members of staff, at the prospect of having his premises patronized by such a distinguished visitor. I already had Floyd cast for the part and now he and the rest of them needed to give a solid performance.

"Please give me a few moments and then make your way down to the lower floor. How many of you are there?"

"Twenty-four."

"*Twenty-four*! Twenty-four, (a little calmer) right sir, just a few minutes, please."

I went back outside and issued quick and specific instructions:

"We're in but I haven't got time to explain. Floyd... You are Chief Malinga of the Sotho tribe. Do not attempt to utter a single word! Understood?"

He replied with a silent nod of his head:

"Don, you are his bodyguard. Angela and the other two ladies are his three wives."

Angela raised just one eyebrow with an icy stare and said:

"Which numbered wife am I?"

I took this sardonic question to mean she was number one and granted her the status. She looked comically smug and gratified.

"What's going on?" uttered one of the hosting Head-teachers.

"No time for that now, only speak when ordering and leave the rest to me. I'm his interpreter, just follow my cues."

I led the party down the stairs to the lower floor where astonishingly, the manager had cleared six tables of their occupants and re-seated them in cramped conditions on tables of two, around the periphery of the room.

He then expressed his profound apologies from the disruption they had endured and announced that everything they had ordered would be on the house!

The six tables of four seats were reconfigured in the middle of the room and we took to our seats, making sure Floyd was positioned at the top seat.

Within a few moments a pleasant young lady came to the table and asked Floyd what he would like:

"We've got some really nice loose-leaf Zulu tea."

I quickly intervened before he could answer. I was well into the roles of producer, director and supporting artist:

"Oh, I am sorry, but protocol dictates that you don't speak directly to the chief. It is considered disrespectful. You can speak through me or his bodyguard."

Angela raised another eyebrow in disbelief; the hosts looked dumbfounded; Don looked down at the table, trying not to laugh and Floyd kept up his deception like... a chief.

"Oh dear," she declared, "I'm so sorry."

"That's alright, you weren't to know." Then she redirected the question back at me.

From my time at Ebony Park School, I had learnt a few

lines from a Zulu hymn and thought now was the time to say them:

"Siyahamb' ekukhanyeni kwenkos Zulu tea." (The translation is 'We are marching in the light of God'.)

To his eternal credit, Floyd nodded his head in a slow, deliberate and regal manner as if to accept the recommendation and the waitress duly scribbled it down on her notepad.

Don was trying to force his own fist into his mouth, as the girl systematically took orders around the table.

"You can talk directly to the wives: that's permitted."

"Thank you."

This time all three sets of eyes from the 'wives' bore through me, accompanied by incredulous looks from the hosts; not to mention the full attention of the entire room.

A little boy came over from one of the displaced families and asked excitedly if Floyd was a real chief. I confirmed he was and asked the youngster if he would like the Chief's signature:

"Yes please."

"Don would you please ask the Chief if he would sign his name on one of these napkins?"

Don, rolling his eyes, said something in Afrikaans to Floyd, who in turn, took a pen from his jacket and autographed the paper. I picked it up and gave it to the boy who went back to his seat. Don then leaned across the table and whispered to me in his distinctive voice:

"Poll...you will go strrraight to Hell, withowt stopping!"

Floyd nodded majestically in agreement. I smiled and winked back.

The Manager eventually came over and to be fair, not once did he engage in any obsequiousness but merely asked Floyd if he was happy with the service:

"Oh, I'm terribly sorry but custom requires that you do not speak directly to the Chief."

"Forgive me; I didn't know."

"Of course you didn't, I'll ask him if he is happy." (Cue another line from 'Siyahamba' ending with 'Betty's'.)

Floyd was still on contract to fulfil his acting obligations and bowed his head once again in the manner of a tribal leader.

Angela raised her eyebrow in disbelief and Don shook his head behind the Manager.

"Many thanks for your visit. Hope to see you again."

When we all got out of the restaurant, Floyd let out a long sigh and asked for permission to speak. One of the Headteachers in a mock reprimand said:

"That was outrageous, Paul. I hope this doesn't get out!"

"It won't, because you're all accomplices!" I replied laughing.

Don reiterated his prediction:

"There'll be no coming back frrrom that hortt place, Paulus!"

We debated on the way home as to whether the Manager should have granted us entry, and whether he might be accused of suffering a little from idolatry or shallowness. I disagreed; I thought he was remarkably resourceful and showed incredible leadership skills under immense pressure.

He didn't suffer any net loss; his establishment entertained a 'distinguished' guest; we paid out a fortune and twenty-four customers got an unexpected free tea! So, pluses all round.

We tried the same ruse at the Leeds Playhouse and as a result, were allowed backstage to meet the cast; though Angela once again, insisted on being the first wife!

We had four more days at school with art, music, religious education, humanities and literacy all benefiting enormously from the South Africans' visit. The displays adorned our walls for some considerable time.

During the mid-weekend, our itinerary took us all to London, where we stayed unexpectedly at the reasonably-priced Tower Bridge Hotel for two nights; unusual given the proximity of this building to its historical namesake.

The following day saw us busily engaged in trying to get our visitors around as many London landmarks as possible. Luckily, the weather was glorious, so walking was the preferred and advantageous option.

What surprised our guests most, were the notorious prices of London. Even the most basic of requirements such as bottled water or coffee were extortionate. It would have cost less to have been the victim of a mugging! So, when we walked past Westminster Abbey and one of the 'wives' made a request to go in, my heart sank when I saw the entry price.

It's well known that South Africans are a devout nation and I knew this opportunity was important to them. I also knew how sensational this group were at gospel singing. They had sung at our initial gathering for this tour and again were dressed accordingly, in their joy-inducing regalia, so befitting for the people of a 'Rainbow Nation'.

I took Don, Angela and Floyd to one side and asked if they would be prepared to sing for their entrance fee. At once they agreed and took up their positions along with the others, on a grassed verge adjacent to the mass of people queuing patiently. They struck up with the beautiful national anthem of their country, which immediately drew the attention of the captive audience.

My goodness me, it sounded wonderful and was well received; the audience clapped appreciatively. They then went on to perform a superb repertoire of gospel songs, which not only appealed to the throng of people waiting but also prompted them to throw money – lots of it! Lis, a Headteacher, used a hat to gather the silver and gold coins that rained down and then went in amongst the crowd to collect more.

Things were going swimmingly well until a 'jobsworth' in a peaked hat with 'Westminster Abbey Warden' on it came over and issued us with a *warning*:

"You can't sing here, busking isn't allowed."

"We didn't come here intending to," I replied, "but we certainly are entertaining those waiting to go in."

People from the queue came over to appeal to the intransigent official who replied:

"It says 'Keep off the Grass', can't you read? If you don't stop, I'll call the police" … which is exactly what he did, despite the collective protestations from onlookers.

The crowd asked the choir to continue, which of course they did.

Presently, along came a policeman who momentarily stood listening to the singing, moving his head to the rhythm and appreciating the spectacle; that is until the warden demanded to know what he was going to do. Even the officer seemed irritated by his abrupt manner.

In fairness, we probably were breaking the *rules*, but I don't know if I was more incensed at his not appreciating the delights of this impromptu performance, or by the 'super-powers' he presumed his hat gave him. From the start, he had been rude to an unpardonable degree and had he been polite, we should have stopped immediately.

The officer was far more pleasant, understanding and I think reluctant in asking us to desist. As the choir stopped the queue of people, including newcomers, applauded.

As events settled down, Lis came back with the total of our bounty. Not only did everyone gain free entry, but there was more than enough left over for a donation to the Abbey!

Chapter Twenty-Two

EXPOSURE

DON WAS not himself on the way back in the coach. Something was troubling him and I wanted to get to the bottom of it. I was aware that we had not been together as much as I had hoped and I desperately wanted him to see my school, staff and pupils with Floyd.

"What's the matter, Big Don?"

"Tch, Paulus, I wish I could stay with you and have more fun," he said rubbing his forehead discontentedly.

"It's like living in a prison with my host. I feel uncomfortable about getting anything out of the cupboards, even a cup."

Her house-pride was driving him to distraction and he didn't feel he could even rearrange the cushions to sit down on the sofa. In addition, he told me that she had organised so many meetings to attend in the evenings, that he had become totally isolated from his colleagues.

"Oh, that's not good, never mind we're all going to the Yorkshire Playhouse Theatre in Leeds on Thursday, so that will be a nice treat."

"Ach! I won't be able to go, Paulus, she's got me booked in for a Governors' meeting that night."

"Well, that's not happening, every one of your colleagues is going, so you shall not be left out."

"No, she insists I attend." He looked so dejected and downhearted that I felt I needed to intervene.

"Right, you *are* going to the theatre with the rest of us. Don't worry I'll sort it out."

I rang the host directly. I didn't know her at all well and had conversations with her only on several occasions, involving small talk. When I put Don's case to her, she was not at all accommodating, but rather insistent that he attend the Governors' meeting. I reiterated the fact that Don would be the only one of twelve visiting Headteachers not attending the theatre. Again, she refused to allow him to miss the arranged meeting.

I put down the phone and contacted a staff member linked to the overseas visit at the Local Authority, who said the matter was out of their hands and down to individual hosts. So, I contacted Don and told him I would pick him up early regardless of what he had been told and take full responsibility for my decision. I did and the South Africans had a fabulous evening. In fairness, they took full advantage of meeting up and conversing in their own tongue, on one of the few dedicated whole group outings.

I eventually got Don back to his host around twelve midnight and told him to be quiet entering, as the house was in darkness. To my astonishment, Don said that he would have to knock as he had not been given a key. I told him I would wait while he did so.

It seemed like an age before lights came on and I saw Don disappear into the house and then went home with Floyd.

The next morning, we arrived early at school, around 7.30 to see Don *sitting on the curb* of the car park, with all his possessions in the drizzly weather, soaked to the skin!

"What's happened, Don?" I enquired quizzically.

"Ach, she threw me out Paulus, because I went to the show against her will."

"What!" I was incandescent with rage and couldn't believe she would do something as drastic or selfish as this.

"She dropped me off half an hour ago and said if I wanted to be with you that much, I'd have to stay at your house."

I could not have been more angry if she had made him walk all the way to my school from the other side of the city.

"You're soaked, man! Let's get you inside, I keep some spare clothes at school in case I can't get back home to change."

He went in and got changed into the ill-fitting clothes until I dried his off in the Nursery.

I gave him my school fleece, which made him feel more comfortable and sat him down to talk to arriving staff, whilst I went off to compile a letter.

Maybe I should have waited to cool down before putting pen to paper, but such was my anger that I wrote the letter there and then and sent it to his host's school. I didn't hold back and complained in the strongest terms, saying she was guilty of causing an international incident. I sent a copy to the then Director of Education and went back to the staffroom.

Staff were making Don feel comfortable and welcome when I came into the room and said:

"Hi Don, so how's 'Blackie'?"

The staffroom fell silent and temporary horror-filled expressions were directed towards me, as anticipated.

"Thank you, Paulus," – Don rolled his eyes up at me – "he's fine and sends you his regards." Realising the staff were feeling slightly uncomfortable, he put them at ease, by saying 'Black' was his name and I had met him on my initial visit to Pretoria.

As primary sources of information and evidence, Floyd and Don visited most year groups providing much entertainment, answering many questions and helping to build up a rich impression of what life was like in their respective schools back home. By the time they had finished, both staff and pupils in Downton Primary considered just how fortunate they were.

All three of us drove home and Gwynneth organised sleeping arrangements, so that Don and Floyd had separate rooms and the kids shared. It was to be the beginning of a long-lasting friendship and multiple trips to and from South Africa.

Confusingly, two days later I received a telephone call from a *male* Headteacher, of the school I presumed Don's host to be. We knew each other, but I was not aware that he was the Principal of this particular school. He was extremely polite, but was concerned that his 'Literacy Coordinator' was off school with 'stress' having received my letter and was putting her union in charge of the matter.

"Literacy Coordinator?" – I inquired – "I thought she was a headteacher."

"Oh no, she took my place on the trip."

"Are you aware of *exactly* what she has done?"

"Yes, I'm afraid I am," (he acknowledged sympathetically) but I'm just warning you of her intentions."

"Thank you, but I'm more concerned about the possible repercussions of what can only be described as an international incident. This visiting headteacher has been thrown out of her house and now feels an overwhelming sense of shame and embarrassment; all this after he bestowed the greatest hospitality and generosity on her."

He agreed that it was a wretched situation but felt it

incumbent upon him to inform me. I thanked him and put down the phone.

As Don was feeling guilty and uneasy over the affair, I contacted the Gauteng Local Authority official who had travelled with the Headteachers, to explain that it was I who took responsibility for his actions that night. He was understanding and assured me that he would not be held responsible back home. I told him that I would deal with the matter after their departure. I shared this information with Don who was somewhat relieved and in a better position to enjoy the last few days.

About a week after the guests had returned home, I had a visit from the Director of Education's press secretary to inform me of his disapproval at being 'copied-in' to my letter of complaint. I said that I was more than happy to meet this matter head-on with union representatives, but should Don's *host* want to take it further, then the Director had to be aware of what was going on and not turn his back on it.

Inevitably, an official letter from this woman's union landed on my desk a couple of days later, demanding an apology from me for causing her distress and time off work. I didn't even bother informing my union but replied with a scathing counter-demand, that she apologise to the L.A. for being involved in a Headteachers' tour without holding the post and through a paucity of experience, wisdom or basic judgement, initiated an international incident. Furthermore, if any apologies were to be extracted, then primarily they should be from her towards Don and his family who welcomed and hosted her at great expense.

Thereafter, nothing was heard from them.

Chapter Twenty-Three

EARTHQUAKE!

THE SUMMER holidays of 2003 brought welcome relief from the pressure of work and the logistical machinations involving the overseas visitors. We were very much looking forward to our two-week holiday in Lefkas.

Having booked a second-storey room at a modestly priced three-star hotel, it wasn't long before we were 'catching rays' beside the communal private pool, overlooking the turquoise sea with the white foaming waves lazily hurling themselves onto the sun-baked sands.

We chose this Ionian island, not only because of its guaranteed weather and relative quietness but also because of a shared love of its food and traditional villages, with their engaging occupants. Another one of its enticing features is – unlike many other Greek islands – the rich and fertile hills and peaks are covered with a carpet of lush vegetation, making them enjoyable to explore.

It is also joined to the mainland by a causeway with a drawbridge, making it one of the few islands you can drive to and from.

After a restful couple of days, we went exploring the shops; we always bring some authentically made souvenirs or kitchenware back. In one shop I noticed a beautifully made glazed olive oil pot, which I picked up and brought to the attention of the non-English speaking shopkeeper. I thought it would be a good idea to purchase some oil to put in it, so I could use it during our stay. Asking the man for some olive oil, he surprisingly had difficulty understanding my request for such a popular condiment, I thought. So, employing the time-honoured, English-traveller's method of communicating abroad, I spoke more slowly with increased volume: "Have you any olive oil?" followed by his putting hands up and shrugging. *"More loudly then,"* I'm thinking.

"Have you any olive oil, OLIVE OIL?"

Still not comprehending. I flippantly said to Gwynneth "I'm going to take out the 'Ls'."

"Have you any oyiv oyo...OYIV OYO!"

"Ahh oyiv oyo, yes oyiv oyo!"

To my utter astonishment and everyone else's profound amusement, he understood me.

Three days into the holiday and I was rudely awoken at 6.00 am. by the headboard banging on the wall...and it wasn't us!

A sound, one might only describe as an express train was coming from beneath the bed. Then shaken out of my early morning stupor, the full might of this shockwave hit us... "Christ, an earthquake!"

I leapt out of bed and was immediately thrown across the room with some considerable force,

Landing in a clump on the floor. I noticed the sink had come away from the wall as I struggled to get to my feet. Entering into the children's sleeping area, I saw both clutching onto the legs of their beds, whilst being bounced around the floor; expressions of fear etched onto their faces.

"Leave everything, let's get out of here!" – was my unwise but forthright command.

The building was now being shaken as if it was a hand-held flexible piece of plastic piping. (I was later to find out this was, luckily intended).

We struggled to make our way down the stairway (another bad decision) and eventually out into the garden, where we joined several other guests in various stages of undress, with one or two screaming.

The shockwave lasted some fifteen seconds, not long relatively speaking, but an absolute age as far as the duration of an earthquake is concerned.

As things settled down and we gradually recovered from the shock and realization of getting caught up in a real demonstration of Mother Nature's awesome power, I went upstairs to get everybody some clothes and after getting dressed, found some refuge in the hotel's garden.

Eventually, I said to Gwynneth that I was going to make my way down to the travel representative's company building, to find out what was going on.

On my way down to the main high street, I became aware of some of the damage caused by the quake. A small, historical stone-built church had been split in two and the main road had a fissure down its entire length as far as I could see, with a river of what appeared to be wine, along with many other escaped bottled juices, disappearing into it! People were frantically running in every direction and a queue of traffic was on the move.

Upon entering the travel firm's building, there was a hive of frenetic activity, with a huge flat-screened television showing newsflashes of a 6.9 earthquake, as measured on the Richter Scale. It didn't take me long to deduce that I was wasting my time trying to get assistance at this point, so made the decision to leave; just at that moment, a huge second shockwave hit. Everyone queuing made a bolt for the doorway. I followed them. As I stepped out of the office to get away from the shaking building, I was suddenly and violently pulled back into the office, by the collar of my shirt! Feeling momentarily disorientated, I suddenly heard my 'assailant's' voice cry out:

"Those people are mad, stand under the lintel of the doorway. It's the safest place if the building collapses."

Clearly, I should have followed the same procedure at the hotel, instead of trying to get out.

"If you go outside now, you are likely to be killed by falling balconies, masonry or cars out of control."

My 'Guardian Angel' stayed with me until the shock-wave subsided, at which point I was completely alone with the staff. After thanking him, I asked what our options were. He directed me to a woman behind the desk.

She said that hundreds of people had left the island via the causeway, in their rented cars to get flights home. There was to be no compensation as it was an 'act of God', so the decision was mine. I glanced at the television screen and for once made an intelligent decision. The second quake had registered 6.5 on the Richter Scale. I said the aftershocks and tremors were decreasing in strength, which appeared to suggest that things were beginning to settle down:

"This holiday has cost us a fair amount and the locals can't just take off and leave everything behind. We're only three days into our stay, but I'm afraid we're not prepared to stay on the second floor of a hotel. Have you an equivalent ground floor option?"

She turned the massive file of places available around and said:

"Take your pick. You can stay at any hotel now, they're all empty! There are some really plush and pleasant five-star accommodations we could transfer you to, without incurring any further charges. This one is the best with all the modern conveniences. Collect your belongings and

I'll let them know you're coming. It's quite close to where you are."

It looked superb and well worth the wait to see if the current situation improved.

I made my way back to the garden where Gwynneth and the children were waiting, with grim-looking expressions. I relayed all the information to her and she bravely agreed to delay our decision to leave.

After convincing the worried three-star hotelier that she would still be paid, we transferred our belongings to the five-star option and decided to take a trip to the coast away from the town – possibly another poor decision.

Following the narrow road to the sea, we had to negotiate a number of rockfalls and wondered if we were being taken into new dangers; not least of all a dreaded tsunami.

Notwithstanding, we parked the car and headed for the quay to purchase some lunch and have a look at the boats.

A short while later, the third earthquake struck! This time white goods, televisions and furniture could be heard and seen bouncing around the insides of apartments, together with the screams of terrified occupants. Then frighteningly, part of the quay cracked and fell away and the road through the village opened along its length.

The most heart-wrenching moment was when a mother in a selfless act, gestured to a boat owner to take her baby away from possible falling masonry. He rather selfishly was more concerned about saving his boat and pulling away from the jetty. The different human responses to the disaster, are forever lodged in my memory. I witnessed brave, selfless, calm and caring acts of humanity, but these were easily eclipsed perhaps understandably, by the more numerous acts of panic, self-preservation and selfish endeavours.

We could see the rising clouds of dust sent high into the air by the 'bouncing' mountain range and decided to quickly return to the hotel garden before we were trapped by falling rock or worse, drowned by a predicted giant wave.

We returned to a large gathering of people ranging from locals, owners, workers and a few guests in the garden, along with bedding and possessions. They were clearly preparing to 'camp out' for the night. Following their cue, we brought bedding from our room and selected a small area to prepare sleeping arrangements. There was a kind of 'Blitz'-camaraderie about the place, especially as aftershocks were occurring on a regular basis. The outside barman was wonderful; assuaging peoples' fears as they rumbled on through the day, by pointing out that it was the Earth's way of settling down.

That night a young four-year-old Harry, resting in my arms rather poignantly and tear-jerkingly asked if I... "could stop the underground thunder."

"I should have been born on Krypton and wear my underpants on the outside, to be able to do that Son, I'm sorry. The remark cheered up some of the worried neighbours at least.

Someone once asked me what it was like to experience an earthquake. Well, even solid ground feels like you're stepping onto a lilo floating on the water. It's terrifying!

The next day we went walking amongst the scenes of carnage. In the local quay, sailing boats had been upended at their moorings and buildings showed signs of movement with cracked rendering and exposed reinforcement bars protruding from their corners. I later learned that this type of construction allows for violent movement in earthquakes and allows for re-rendering should it be necessary. The design certainly saved many lives that day, with no recorded related deaths. And so it should have, as it became standard procedure in the building trade after the last earthquake which killed up to an estimated eight hundred people. That was exactly fifty years before... *to the day*, on August 14th 1953.

To take the family's mind off the frightful events, I hired a large sailing boat and skipper for the day to enable Gwynneth especially – a competent sailor – the chance of helming. Money was no longer an issue as I realised there were no shops in the afterlife.

We had a remarkable day sailing to and swimming off the island of Skorpios, owned by the Onassis family. Our skipper was a young but talented sailor and introduced us to places we should never have seen. The only downside of an otherwise amazing day was that Harry got stung by a wasp and 'danced' around the deck softly and pathetically crying "Oh gosh, oh gosh!" Feeling his pain, I said to Gwynneth that he was reluctant to blasphemously cry out 'Oh God' as I should have irreverently done so. Luckily, a kind woman was on hand to give assistance with some sting cream when we quayed at a divine-looking village. So, it looks as if he did respond to the cries for help. She wouldn't have been there if it had happened to me.

We spent the rest of our time wondering if more earthquakes would come, with me insisting that we slept with the lights on in case we needed a hasty retreat to the nearest lintel.

The five-star Hotel was nice though.

Chapter Twenty-Four

CREVASSE

WE ONCE had a child with 'Fragile X Syndrome': a genetic disorder which prevents the normal development of the brain. Some of the associated difficulties include social and behaviour problems, learning disabilities and developmental delays in basic functions.

As well as these challenging characteristics, he also had Tourette's which meant he could be quite a handful for his carer.

He was often prone to soiling himself but because of his condition, was neither able to prevent it nor give warning of his need to use the lavatory.

I was very reticent about using the Gents at school for a sit-down performance, as it were, because the facility had been upgraded to accommodate disabled access as well as public use.

In addition, there were always interruptions or seamless demands on my time. Nevertheless, on one occasion, I found myself unable to resist this particular law of nature.

Having luckily survived 'the ordeal' without disturbance, I was acutely aware that the little room perhaps needed more than the customary 'five minutes'. It was definitely a 'Pepé Le Pew' moment.

I surreptitiously left the scene of crime and retreated to my office, no more than a few metres away.

A few minutes later, a very concerned carer came to me and said that Lionel had to go home because he had messed himself:

"Are you quite sure he requires sending home, we have had false alarms before?"

His carer exclaimed:

"I've just allowed him to use the adult toilet and after following him in there was no doubt; it was *awful!*"

"Oh dear!" I replied... "You'd better contact his mother."

She dutifully rang.

As Lionel got older, his condition became worse and not least of all because his older brother and associates were encouraging him to use unacceptable language. The upshot of this situation meant on occasions, he required two carers and staff were continually sending him on errands to the secretaries' office or trips to the library.

I was in the main office one afternoon talking to my Business Manager when Lionel appeared at the hatch. She got up to assist and followed the protocol of making a fuss of him, to keep him 'on side':

"Hello, Lionel. How are you today, is that note for me?"

"Yeah, yeah, note for you."

"Well thank you for bringing it to me."

"would you like a nice biscuit?"

"Yeah, yeah, I wanna nice biscuit."

"You'll have to follow me to the staffroom, that's where they are. I'll let you in this once, because you're not allowed in on your own, (*to the elephants' sacred, burial ground*) are you?"

"No, no, not allowed...biscuit, biscuit, yeah, yeah!"

My Business Manager opened the door and went ahead of him, encouraging Lionel to follow her. I went along also, with the intention of continuing our meeting over a cup of tea.

As she made her way down the corridor, towards the staffroom door, Lionel swung his arm and slapped her on the backside with considerable force. A piercing shriek was emitted by the woman and Lionel responded with:

"Well get a fucking move on then!"

She turned to me with a face like thunder and flushed with embarrassment:

"Well, aren't you going to say something!?"

"You know Lionel, I've been wanting to do that for an awfully long time."

Judging by her expression, I knew immediately there would be retribution for that comment later.

That retribution came in the form of a divine response, when later that term I was giving a guided tour of our displays and ICT capabilities to the local vicar, a group of headteachers and another school's Chair of Governors.

I was proudly walking through our shared open space, drawing attention to various points of discussion, when inevitably we entered the newly upgraded library; only to see Lionel simulating the role of the librarian, who was there, showing him how books were lent out.

At that moment, my heart froze and realising that the situation could escalate into an awkward encounter, chose not to engage Lionel in conversation. Instead, I walked on with my colleagues, trying to avoid eye contact. Then the anticipated, ineluctable dulcet tones seemed to fill the entire building:

"Oi, Franklin, you complete wanker!"

Gasps of shock came from my guests as well as from children being served in the library. All at once, the whole place fell silent and I felt everyone's gaze 'burn' into me, as they awaited my response to the torrent of abuse. I could think of only one reply:

"I'm inclined to agree with you Lionel, but who are we against so many?"

Of course, it was completely lost on our 'little angel' who stared at me with equal amounts of confusion and intent, but the answer wasn't intended for him anyway.

The visiting party roared with laughter and I quickly ushered them out of the area before he could say anything else.

Chapter Twenty-Five

ESSENTIAL MOTIVATION

READING IS always set and encouraged by teachers as homework from the earliest years, because it is the necessary building block of learning and pervasive means of communication in any subject. As children enter Key Stage One and Two especially, they are expected to carry out writing and research exercises at home, simply to reinforce learning concepts and allow the teacher to make assessments of a pupil's progress and understanding.

It is not good enough for teachers to presume children are defying their wishes to complete tasks. Indeed, there are many complex reasons as to why children fail to produce the brief or expected outcomes. For example, children may be part of a large family in cramped or shared living conditions, where noise, disruption and financial difficulties prevent extended periods of study. Some children may live in fear of punishment for not completing tasks set at home; others may be discouraged by parents because they can't help or don't believe in its use. Commonly, the responsibilities of being a carer may rest upon the shoulders of surprisingly young individuals. Ian however was just spoilt, lazy and defiant. I had occasional arguments with his mother because she didn't agree with our methodologies. She even accused me once of not knowing what I was doing, to which I replied:

"To be a Headteacher, one needs to pass many qualifications and tests, whilst accumulating much experience in various settings, over a lengthy time period. On the other hand, to be a parent, one only needs to know how to reproduce and there are no exams in that!" (Thanks to Rick for the quote.)

Unsurprisingly, the argument escalated into a crescendo of 'tit-for-tat' insults, the last of which I shouted down the corridor, as she steamed out of my office; much I suppose, in the manner of Jeremy Clarkson:

"You are the worst parent *in the world*!"

However, teachers throughout his passage of education were at a loss as to how they could deal with his reluctance to participate. They tried keeping him in at breaktimes (after school wasn't an option), having his parents in and denying privileges.

In Year Six, his teacher was worried that our percentages for 'Level Four' 'SAT' results would be detrimentally affected, if we couldn't raise his assessment results; something he was more than capable of doing. I asked her to leave the problem with me to ponder over.

That Friday, I stayed behind to catch up with some work, after everyone else had gone. Come six-o-clock, I was tired and wanted to get back home to the family but instead drove to Ian's home.

I knocked purposefully on the door and a surprised and bewildered Ian opened it.

"Mr Franklin, what are you doing here?"

"I've come to help you with your homework. Are your mum and dad in?"

"Yes," he replied, struggling to swallow.

"Good, well aren't you going to invite me in?"

I entered the front room and politely greeted the equally bemused parents, informing them that I was going to help Ian get a top grade for his homework that week.

I pointed out that he was a capable boy who was under-performing and with my help he could easily achieve the best marks in the class. They liked that and it set the tone for 'burying the hatchet.'

His mother cleared the table in the dining area and we sat alongside each other working for ninety minutes. Ian completed the work himself, with some guidance. The most extraordinary event for me was how his parents accessed reference books and a dictionary to help their son.

It was a pleasant session and Ian ended up quite proud of his achievements. He even acknowledged the benefits of completing his homework on a Friday evening, to leave the rest of the weekend free for leisure pursuits-in the form of unsociable behaviour, no doubt.

I didn't arrive home until 8.45 that evening but felt 'Operation Essential Motivation' had been a complete success. There was still one more action I needed to undertake, in order to achieve the best results.

At the end of the Monday morning assembly before pupils went off to their lessons, I politely asked Ian to stand up so that everybody could hear him answer my question:

"Ian, would you mind telling everyone where I was on Friday evening?"

(*Reticently and quietly*) "At my house."

"Do you think you could speak just a little more loudly?"

(*Louder*) "At my house."

"Did you know I was coming to see you at home?"

"No!"

"Why did I come and visit you then?"

"Because I hadn't done my homework." (*Gasps from the school.*)

"So, because you hadn't done your homework, I came to visit and what did I do?"

"You sat at our table and stayed to help me for nearly two hours." (*More gasps of surprise.*)

"Well Ian, do you have any advice that you'd like to share with the rest of the school?"

"Make sure you do your homework or Mr Franklin will come round."

"One last thing Ian, I'm going to ask your teacher to give me the results of your homework, so that we may share them with the rest of the school tomorrow – OK?" (*He nodded.*)

The following morning, I asked Ian to stand up again but this time to make his way to the front. I announced his grade and asked the whole school to applaud, then gave him a Headteacher award sticker. All primary school children love stickers.

He at once became flushed with pride and smiled at the attention he was receiving this time. I winked at him as he left the hall.

We lasted a full half-term without incident, regarding homework submissions from the *whole* school, out of that little manoeuvre.

Chapter Twenty-Six

HOSTILE AND CHALLENGING CLIMATE

ALL SCHOOLS have recorded incidences of bullying, racism and to some extent gender-stereotyping, although the latter to a less extent in an age of 'Woke' culture and equality. In primary education, it's not unusual to hear of mixed-gender sports teams or interchangeable acting roles for example.

Sadly, bullying and racism are tougher nuts to crack as they are behaviourally learned and transferable traits. Very often, I've heard children repeat narrow-minded, inexcusable 'soundbites', or ignorant opinions they've adopted from family relatives.

My intense disliking of bullying and racism is born out of personal experience and not just whilst visiting South Africa.

For five long years, I was bullied at secondary school; not because I was passive or submissive, but because I was well-built, strong and regarded as a 'line of defence' to be attacked or breached. I wasn't alone. An equally formidable black friend of mine was also a victim of constant racial abuse, because like me he championed the underdog and just wanted to apply himself to work and achieve. We eventually 'teamed up' as it were, to protect each other, when individual bullies formed alliances and attacked in 'wolf-packs'.

Altercations were almost daily events with 'knuckle-scaping, brick-brain' louts, lining up alongside each other and encouraging their neer-do-wells to bring down the victims. The problem was my friend and I couldn't permanently be together, as our lesson studies didn't always coincide.

One of the favourite pastimes of the bully was to shut down lathes by pressing emergency cut-outs in the metalwork lessons, thus damaging work in progress. This was frequently followed by a 'shower' of swarf thrown over the head of the operator from behind. When one turned around there was always a line of 'laughing-hyenas' pointing to other pupils as the perpetrator.

Over time, this behaviour not only psychologically affected me but wore down my resilience.

It eventually reached a critical point one Monday afternoon in the Fifth Year or Year Eleven as it is now. Unusually and inexplicably, I walked the mile-and-a-half home for lunch that day, with my head full of ominous thoughts. I remember entering the kitchen, making a cup of tea and spooning six helpings of sugar into it; strange, because I didn't take sugar! I gulped down the remedial warm beverage, having not had lunch and went back to school almost immediately, knowing my state of mind was a portent of an approaching storm. The nightmare was going to end during this particular afternoon as a conflict was inevitable, if not unavoidable.

After registration, I entered into the metalwork lesson and set up my work on the lathe. The atmosphere was electrically charged, as if my potential assailants knew this moment was pivotal in their campaign of terror.

As I set about turning a piece of aluminium, I was showered in a mix of filthy detergent and metal filings, covering my hair and clean, white shirt. Although expected, I was partially shocked by the cold waste enveloping me and felt a tingling sensation as I turned to face a group of grinning jackals. I focused my eyes on one of them, he had been a recurring bane.

I purposefully walked towards him devoid of any worry for my safety or resulting consequences. An adrenalin-fuelled, left-handed punch that I never felt – in a momentary out-of-body experience – struck him on the jaw and sent him staggering backwards across the room; his head sickeningly striking a metal cupboard. Almost in slow motion he slid down its door, landing in a crumpled, motionless heap on the floor.

"You're dead now Franklin!" … came the threat from one of his cronies; though it mattered not because an increased charge of strength was now coursing throughout my body. I had stepped beyond the threshold of caring, fear or sensibility. I only recognised the primordial instinct of fight or flight and I embraced the former. No one amongst the chattering pack of 'hyenas' was bold or daring enough to approach me. My stare burned into the bloodied face of a slowly recovering adversary; his head held in the arms of a follower. For the very first time I saw abject fear in his eyes; the moment of realization that his reign of terror had culminated in this 'reaping of the whirlwind'.

The teacher was very quickly on the scene and was administering first aid whilst commanding a colleague to call for an ambulance. Still, the baying pack was issuing threats to an oblivious target.

The ambulance was very quick on the scene and soon my opponent was being stretchered into the back of the vehicle, parked on the school's playground. To the ever-increasing crescendo of threats, I was escorted to the office of the staff member as the class was dismissed.

"I never knew it was as bad as this, Paul," said a worried and concerned Mr Bowden.

I can remember repeating over again, in a shaking, post-traumatic trance-like state:

"I just wanted to be able to do my work."

In what seemed to be a long time later, I was escorted to the Headteacher's office; a place I'd never been before in five years! Mr Williams was a kind and understanding man, who acknowledged how much I and so many others had been provoked by this group of individuals. He kindly told me that I was not in trouble and that he had contacted my father to collect me, as he was worried about likely retaliations after school. As I left the building, my then English teacher thanked me and promised to buy me a drink!

I never saw the individual I struck in school again. It was near the end of term in any case. However, the following week at the same time-tabled lesson, an individual called Mick was coaxed into confronting me by his reluctant friends. He did so with a screwdriver.

Suppressing the rage that I could feel returning, I remember the cold warning I gave out.

"You're going to look awfully silly, with that sticking out of your arse Mick!"

He put down the tool and walked away. My only regret was that I hadn't made a stand five years earlier. When I became a head this recurring memory of deep-seated suffering and regret, was the driving force behind my protection of similar victims of bullying.

I used to make announcements to classes or whole-school congregations, that I had befriended certain individuals experiencing intimidation and that I would consider an attack on them as one on me. That was an effective ploy in school, but not always outside of it.

One very worried parent came to see me and explained

that whilst her son was only, but often being verbally harassed on the journey to and from home, it was much worse during other times. I made it clear to parents that I had jurisdiction over those carrying out threats to others whilst wearing school uniform, but it was more difficult for me to police out-of-school hours, such as weekends or holidays.

Nevertheless, my advice to her was both unorthodox and yet supportive. Her lad was passive during confrontations, not an unworthy trait but not always the best ploy. He was going to invite further intimidation unless he put up some act of resistance. My advice to her was to encourage him to 'bare his teeth' if he found himself under threat:

"Do you understand what I'm not saying?"

"Yes, but what happens if he does this in school?"

"I know your son very well. He would only do this under extreme provocation, so I would view his position sympathetically. I'm not advocating aggression, but sometimes people can demonstrate their unwillingness to accept bullying.

She left in a pensive though committed state of mind. Her son would take some persuading. However, he was confronted in the playground a few days later. He forcibly grabbed his aggressor, but it was not his physical response that frightened a shocked intimidator. It was the way he sinisterly warned him with a spittle-spattered barrage of words through gritted teeth.

Inevitably, they were both sent to me. The bully got short shrift with a warning of exclusion, which incidentally was later imposed in a totally unrelated incident. The other lad got my admiration. His mother was relieved when I saw her next.

Such is my abhorrence of bullying and terror, I'd like to think I would go to someone's aid if they required it, despite living in an age when armed crime is on the increase and few people can overcome their reluctance, to become involved. We should follow the example of the elderly; many of them it seems, possess the mindset to offer resistance, even if it is with just umbrellas or hand-bags!

Chapter Twenty-Seven

A RAY OF SUNSHINE

MOST NEWLY appointed Headteachers inherit their staff. Whilst some are already excellent and dependable, or with experience and training become so, others are unworthy, unreliable and even dishonest. So, when a new secretary was required, my office staff and I thought hard about the practical tests we might employ to get the right candidate. Out of six applicants, we finally narrowed our sights on two obvious choices. In the end, it came down to maths and the combined scores of multiple tests. This was unfortunate because my gut feeling was to choose the person who came in as runner-up. Although she didn't score quite as many points, she possessed more of a warm, engaging personality and professional disposition than the one who was appointed who incidentally like her partner on site, became dishonest and untrustworthy, which ultimately led to their dismissals.

So, it *was* with a heavy heart that I contacted Penny to inform her that she had been unsuccessful in securing the position, but she had been shortlisted to the final two candidates.

A couple of days later, I received a touching hand-written letter from her informing me that she had thoroughly enjoyed the interview and expressed gratitude for the opportunity. It was the first and only time during my senior management years, that I had received a letter of thanks from an applicant who I had turned down. Such was the sincere feeling within the content of her correspondence, I convened a meeting with my Business Manager, to see if it was financially viable to create a position for her. We agreed that the school required someone to run the recently expanded library and perhaps cover absences from the office. I informed Governors and brought her back in before some other intuitive employer got to her before me. To be honest, she had great interactive and communicative skills, which led her to become the 'face' of our school and the first person that parents would be greeted by. Her soft, informative and calming tones often defused difficult and heated confrontations. She was one of only several administrative staff I line-managed who possessed these rare qualities. Devorah was another who rose from the ranks of voluntary assistant to office manager and possessed an entertaining sense of humour.

On reflection and if I could have, there is no doubt that I would have made a handful of auxiliary staff, non-teaching deputies, because they were outstandingly loyal and professional in their positions. They also shared one common denominator…I appointed and promoted them!

Over the course of twenty years, I've received and perused an incalculable number of applications, ranging from the sublime to the 'laugh out loud'. Generally, the worst types have come from under-graduates applying in the spring, for positions available at the start of the new academic year.

Inexperienced and poorly advised students often rely on what I would call the 'Sperm Approach', whereby they write one application and send it off to many schools, hoping for it to 'hit home'. On several occasions I have received bland, word-processed letters, addressed to another headteacher. When this happened, I reduced the number of potential interviewees by simply throwing these ones straight in the bin!

Other students, who happened to get my name right, would offer average skills and try to bolster their chances by saying that they had a 'good deal of experience in...' Hold it right there! You might have experience in playing the piano or recorder, (good additional skills) sailing or even growing mushrooms, (I honestly received the latter) but you do not have vast experience in the maturation process, child psychology or miscue analysis. So, bugger off!

The one big mistake nearly all under and indeed post-graduates made, was to keep using the wrong pronoun – 'I' – the First Person, instead of 'You' – the Second Person'. I would receive a list of things people had done... I did this, I did that, I did the other, instead of you did this, you did that et cetera.

Such was my disappointment at receiving such impersonal and poorly drafted letters, that I contacted several of our feeder universities and asked if I could offer tutorials or lectures on the 'art' of writing applications. Many colleagues of mine had expressed similar views, so I knew the current thinking behind preferred submissions and acceptances.

My advice to students was simple. Target one school and research it thoroughly; by which I mean, its strengths, weaknesses and intentions based on the most recent Ofsted findings.

Point out what the school has achieved, congratulate them and inform the Head where your skills or educational philosophy may fit into their ideas and aspirations. Don't be afraid to highlight or ask the interviewing panel where they believe the school's weaknesses lay. For example, if the school is underperforming in an area of study that is one of your strengths, outline how you may assist the school in overcoming its problems.

Always conclude any answer to a question put to you with 'Have I fully answered your question?'; thus, denying the panel the opportunity to say you didn't during a disappointing feedback session.

If a school is reluctant to give you their current development plan, new staff support packs or discuss their Ofsted outcomes – which are online anyhow – then be wary.

Always' make time to visit the school before an interview in order to see the standard of displays, classwork and behaviour. Talk to pupils and staff at breaktimes and the caretaker, cleaners and parents at home-time. Gradually build up a realistic, rather than advertising profile. Much of the mood of an establishment may be gleaned by these methods.

Finally, accompany your word-processed application with a short, hand-written letter to thank the Head for their time and any literature they may have given you. This fulfils two vital objectives: Firstly, to show you have manners and pleasant social intercourse and secondly, to show that you can write legibly and spell correctly.

The most amusing and audacious submission I received on an official application form, was from a grandmother who admitted to not possessing a degree but thought the experience of looking after her grandchildren, would be enough to warrant her becoming a teacher. Previous experience involved working in a bakery and that was it. Nice try!

Chapter Twenty-Eight

UNEXPECTED OBSTACLES

IN 2007 Ofsted returned and along with the inspection came an inevitable change in people's mood and the working atmosphere. To a large extent, the impromptu nature of the new framework was welcomed more than the previous arrangements, which gave schools a six-week warning, enabling a build-up of tension and anxiety. From a senior manager's point of view, a weekend's notice was often not enough time to 'iron out' any perceived shortfalls or bring to fruition ongoing initiatives which one desperately might want inspectors to see.

The short notice inspections were responsible for the only times I saw staff working in school at weekends. It was a case of all hands on deck!

As usual, I wanted to be observed along with my staff, to underpin the validity of my own monitoring. This time I planned a bold year-group 'Inspire' geography lesson to sixty-plus children and their parents in the hall. The topic was to discuss the importance of quarrying.

Some months before, I had been invited to a 'Redland' presentation on the importance of quarrying and the lengths to which companies went to restore the landscape after their extractions.

To be honest, I was probably guilty of being a 'Nimby' (Not in my backyard) until I was able to witness for myself, the importance of mining or quarrying and the extent to which restoration often led to an improvement of the original or scarred landscape.

As well as our life-dependency on quarries, I was also impressed by the laws that govern this industry and protect wildlife. I was taken to a site where work had temporarily ceased to allow sand martins to nest. At another location, I witnessed the remarkable remedial work that had transformed a working quarry into an educational nature reserve with on and off-land leisure pursuits.

My presentation on quarries needed to be interesting, informative and above all persuasive, so I sought the invaluable support of my Site Supervisor, who helped me gather together as many building materials as possible, comprising different types of sand, aggregates, cement, brick, piping, glass and stone. To these, I added such items as toothpaste, tablets, bread, cereal paper and tinned sardines.

To a packed hall of attentive pupils, parents and two inspectors busily scribbling notes, I put my lesson into context with the moral issues surrounding the tragedy of Aberfan, which occurred on that fateful day – 21st October 1966. I remember the disaster so vividly as a child, not least for witnessing my Mother break down in tears as we watched miners and volunteers dig frantically to rescue or retrieve the bodies of children and staff, from a crushed school entombed in the by-product waste of a mining industry.

So, the question was: "Should we stop this kind of mining, if so or if not why? Discuss.

Inspectors appreciated the fast-paced nature of lessons, not stymied by the droning tones of teachers who love the sound of their own voices. Investigative and pupil discussion-based learning was the preferred model of teaching.

Parents and children understood the necessity of mining or quarrying but safety had to be an issue and this finding led to a brief discussion on governmental measures put into place after this preventable accident.

Next, the parents and pupils were asked to view the array of materials and products on the centre trestle and record on a table of two columns, which of them had or had not been extracted from a quarry. This exercise even got the inspectors involved, because I had asked one or two reliable pupils to approach and invite them to do so. There was no point in them swanning off to put other staff under pressure when I had spent so long preparing for this lesson. True, some staff, myself included, were disappointed when carefully planned lessons were not observed by inspectors. However, under new guidelines staff pretty much knew when they were to be 'targeted'.

This was an enjoyable task and whilst some of the more obvious and easily identifiable products of quarrying were defined, others required discussion; all were categorised.

Then came the results, for partners and groups to tick off. When we got down to the last few items, the exercise became interesting, because toothpaste, tablets and bread all contain chalk (calcium) for abrasion, minerals and drug absorption. This left two products; the sardines, which of course were packed in a metal tin and the packet of Weetabix.

"For God's sake, surely I've got one right. The Weetabix came from a farm, factory and supermarket," said a frustrated grandparent.

"Yes indeed, but that farmland might be on a restored quarry site and the cereals that make up that product would have drawn up minerals from the land." A round of applause and positive acknowledgements from the inspectors ensured the lesson was graded as 'Excellent'. The supportive comments from the elderly gentleman and other parents expressing their enjoyment almost certainly helped.

The 'Inspire' programme was definitely a game-changer, but once again it certainly emphasises just how important the support and harnessed skills from parents and industry are, in terms of the school and their children's development. I deeply valued these partnerships.

When the proposed building of a factory was planned within the school's village, the expected wave of protest from residents, focused upon the perceived disruption from lorries travelling to and from the site and the noise of construction. It was a children's playground equipment manufacturer! Seizing an opportunity to benefit the school, I made an appointment to talk to the owner. He was immensely grateful when I offered to promote the advantages of his business in my newsletter, regarding the employment benefits and the provision of free local play equipment that he had agreed to. This led to a smoother chain of events in the development of his business, but also provided the school with new and influential Governors as well as an array of play equipment for the school. Indeed, it was agreed that our school would become a testing ground for newly designed products. This was a positive link with industry, duly noted by Ofsted and not a few jealous Headteacher colleagues.

Chapter Twenty-Nine

UP IN THE JET STREAMS

DURING THE summer break of 2007, I took the family to South Africa for the first time following an invitation from Don and his wife Valery. After the lengthy journey, Don picked us up from Johannesburg Airport and drove us to Pretoria where they lived. Their house was a dominating feature – a palace if you will. Don advised us to move there with Sterling so strong against the Rand:

"Ach, with the value of yourrrr house, Paulus, you could buy something much bigger here with the currrent exchange rate. You get so much less for yourrr Pound in the UK."

I have to say, a tempting prospect, but with a nine and sixteen-year-old established in their respective schools, not to mention a wife embedded in hers, it was very unlikely to happen.

Don and Valery very kindly gave up their bedroom and en suite for the duration of our three-week stay, in much the same way as they did for the visiting host that threw poor Don out of her house. One unexpected outcome was a house assistant who cooked and washed clothes for us. She was a kind, hard-working lady who we felt obliged to pay extra, despite her protestations.

Over the first few days we acclimatised ourselves to seamless sunshine and heat. We hadn't worn shorts or bathing wear for so long a period of time, much to the bafflement of Don. The irony of this was that we were visiting during their winter season and they dressed accordingly, because they felt cold. To us, it was like a British heatwave.

It was wonderful to see my friends again; Cycil, Handsome, (Victor) and their partners. We revelled in their generous hospitality and genuinely felt at home with them all. Then a few days later, an all-too-familiar event took place involving a firearm. A very disturbed and shaken Cycil, arrived at Don's house one morning. He had been out running earlier that day and had been held up by a desperate black male. He stripped Cycil of his belongings and forced him at gunpoint to give over his wedding ring. According to his recollection, Cycil had great difficulty in removing it, as his fear-induced sweating had swollen his fingers. He was visibly shaking as he conveyed his expectation of being shot! It had been a terrifying moment and certainly highlighted the gun crime that is rife in South Africa.

The following day the whole group looked forward to a Sun City outing. Naturally, the topic of conversation on the journey centred around Cycil's gun incident, but during the course of events, this was temporarily forgotten as we walked around the luxury resort and crossed the Bridge of Time to the Lost City.

The Palace of the Lost City is indeed impressive. It is set on the highest viewpoint in the city surrounded by lush botanical gardens, sculpture-lined pathways and ribbon-like streams that lead down to the Valley of the Waves.

Not wanting to miss the opportunity to see the opulent interior, I asked Don if we could go inside for a peek at this royal building.

"Ach Paulus, You might be able to but they wouldn't let us in."

"Don't talk rot Don, we'll all get in. Let me drive the van."

I pulled into the lavish forecourt of the hotel and at once was stopped by an attendant carrying a clipboard with a long list of expected guests. I was just going to try and appeal to this gentleman's better judgement, when I caught sight of a guest's name on his paperwork, with a visible estimated time of arrival next to it, several hours later.

"That's me Mr (whoever it was) and we're a little early."

"Would you like us to take your luggage inside sir?"

"Not just yet thank you, we would like to have a brief look around first."

"Certainly sir, if you would kindly give me your van keys, I'll ensure it is parked in the reserved place."

"Thank you, my man, that's very helpful."

As we disembarked everyone was trying to process what had just taken place and Don remarked:

"Ach, Paulus Maximus, I've told you where you arrre headed." The name stuck!

We spent the best part of an hour looking around the luxurious and palatial building and when we decided to leave, I asked someone else for the keys to the vehicle. We had a lovely day.

A few more days at Don's and then as previously mentioned, we travelled down to the Kruger National Park as a special treat for Gwynneth and the kids.

On our way home we stopped at a place where some street artists were sculpturing away and Gwynneth fell in love with a huge elephant that had been superbly fashioned out of a single piece of wood. It certainly was impressive and I wondered how on earth we would get it home. It would later provide me with a challenge...

Halfway through our stay, Floyd had arranged some

accommodation for us, in order to take us to the 'Cradle of Humankind' and Soweto. The latter was the epicentre of the struggle against the cruel 'apartheid' regime but was famously known as the home of two Nobel Peace Prize winners, who lived on the same street. We visited the houses of both Nelson Mandela and Desmond Tutu. I'm glad that we went to Soweto, because during my childhood it was always considered a place of unrest and dangerous for white visitors. Some parts are still regarded as no-go areas, but doesn't that relate to most cities? Soweto now appreciates the vital income that tourism brings and whilst we were there, the construction of a new football stadium was in progress, ready for the 2010 World Cup tournament.

Our visit to The Hector Pieterson Museum, named after the twelve-year-old who was shot dead during the well-documented Soweto uprising, was a humbling and heart-rending experience. On the 16th of June 1976, a march took place, involving an estimated two-thousand black schoolchildren protesting against the implementation of Afrikaans and English as the primary languages of instruction; a law passed with scant regard for local or tribal tongues.

What started as a peaceful protest, soon escalated into a bloodbath, leaving ten dead and hundreds injured. It is known that a boy called Hastings Ndlovu was killed first but Pieterson's death was captured by photographers. The handling of this protest provoked international outcries. A visit to their graves in the Avalon Cemetery brought tears of sympathy to our eyes.

On our way into the museum, I was badgered by a street salesman trying to sell me something I didn't particularly want. Nonetheless, I asked the vendor to wait until after our visit, by which time I thought he would have given up on the transaction. How wrong was I? He was still waiting a good two hours later when we emerged, so I gladly purchased his trinket out of appreciation for his doggedness and determination.

For all of us, the most profound experience of the day was a visit to a shantytown organised spontaneously by Floyd as we drove by. Floyd approached a woman who he regarded as a matriarch figure and offered her some money for us to gain entry. With her permission came provisos from Floyd which demanded that we stay with him throughout and leave high-value items out of sight in the car; including cameras, watches and sunglasses. There was little point in reminding them of their poverty. To this day, we have not witnessed worse or even similar cases of destitution and such inhumane levels of deprivation.

Soweto is a different place today but one headline in the *New York Times* is quoted as saying: 'Soweto, Once Unified Against Apartheid, Is Now Divided by Wealth.'

Although not unique by any standards, the antithesis of wealth and extreme poverty is certainly apparent in this city, let alone in South Africa.

The very next day Floyd drove us to the Cradle of Humankind, about thirty miles from Johannesburg. It is situated in the Sterkfontein valley, which lies in both Western Gauteng and the North-West Province. It is so called because the earliest remains of hominids – a group consisting of all modern and extinct 'Great Apes' – were found here. It is believed they date to over three million years ago. 'Mrs Ples' is the name given to the most complete skull found by Robert Broom in 1947. I say the most complete skull, but ironically, Broom blew it into pieces with his 'delicate' use of explosives and a pickaxe! Unsurprisingly, some fragments are missing, but will probably turn up in another district, claiming to be the earliest site of humankind. Funny how four-fifths of

Broom's name spells 'Boom' and four-fifths of nothing is what he nearly ended up with. Thankfully, archaeological digs today are excavated with a little more care, but don't forget that even 'Otzi The Iceman' – found in the Alps and believed to have lived between 3400 and 3100 BCE – was initially pulled about by alpine walkers using their snow poles!

We spent a little time in Durban with Don and company, before flying down to Cape Town. Durban is also known as 'South Africa's Playground' because the weather here is always pleasant and warmer than anywhere else in the country. Some of the best beaches can be found here; the 'Golden Mile' amongst them, with its beautiful sands and lazy-waving palm tree fronds. Not much further into KwaZulu-Natal, there are some game reserves and the rising dark 'Drakensberg' or Dragon Mountains.

Don had very kindly organised a stay for us at the home of a Headteacher colleague called Trevor in Cape Town. We spent three days with him, visiting many tourist sights and the wine district, where we were treated to some wonderful cultural displays and performances, as well as imbibing fine quality labels at a fraction of their cost in the UK.

For me, one of the most memorable and profound experiences we had, was when Trevor took us to the supermarket in his 'Coloured District'. It was during the evening and we were literally the only white shoppers in a busy store. Gwynneth and Harry's sun-bleached blond hair and pale complexions made them stand out amongst the locals, making them feel both conspicuous and 'vulnerable'. So many kind and interested parties came and spoke to us, but more importantly, we all now empathetically understood the possible thoughts and feelings of ethnic-minority children in our schools. How brave the 'Windrush' generation must have been?

Arriving back at Pretoria, I was now faced with the challenge of getting 'Handsome' home. He was so big and I worried about the prospect of having to leave him behind. Once again, most of my clothes were left behind in order to fit him into my suitcase and the remaining socks and underwear were beneficially used to protect his, rather than my extremities.

Eventually, after much adjustment and difficulty in closing the luggage. I heaved the cargo into the car and we left for the airport.

We said our fond farewells to Don, Cycil, Victor and partners, knowing they would be returning to us in four months' time for Christmas and eventually made our way to the 'check-in' desk, with little time to spare. When I placed my suitcase onto the conveyor belt the assistant said it was too heavy. I questioned this and said that we had not exceeded our allotted baggage weight. To this she agreed but pointed out that single cases had a weight limit to protect baggage handlers from possible injury.

"Possible injury? I exclaimed. I managed to lift it easily (I lied) onto the conveyor belt. Who have you got working behind there, Snow White and The Seven Snowflakes?"

"You'll have to take some of the weight out and put it into another bag."

"Have I got time to do that?"

"If you hurry sir."

Well, socks and pants don't weigh much, but luckily the elephant's tusks were removable, so I ran as fast as I could to a luggage shop on the other side (naturally) of the airport.

Racing back with the announcement of our departure gate opening, ringing in my ears, I eventually got back to Gwynneth and the kids, in much the same state I presume as Roger Bannister after his four-minute mile run. Bathed in sweat and cursing repeatedly, I hurriedly repackaged the cases and handed them in; just tipping the scales and managing to get to the gate before it closed. As we boarded the aircraft, I couldn't help but notice it was a Jumbo jet.

Chapter Thirty

UNEXPECTED DEEP SNOW

DON RETURNED with his family and friends four months later, to work in school at the end of the autumn term and to spend Christmas with us. He brought a special surprise guest with him – Zulu Chief Masipe Matlou.

For the week leading up to the holiday break, the Chief led assemblies and classroom workshops in both the Primary and Upper Schools. These involved some fascinating presentations with video footage whilst dressed in stunning tribal costume, relating to historical facts about the KwaZulu-Natal region. His knowledge of Shaka, a Zulu chief and founder of the Zulu empire, was particularly interesting. He was entertaining, informative and very approachable. Again, some extraordinary work and displays came out of his time with children of all ages. They adored him.

With the kind and generous support of friends and additional school funding, all the visitors were allocated accommodation but were brought together as a group each day. The Local Authority provided me with appropriate transport, in the form of a minibus for them to travel together.

Overnight on their day of arrival, we had some significant snowfall in the hills and this led to excitement for some of the visitors the next morning, who had never experienced walking through it. After numerous requests to drive them to the winter wonderland before school, I carefully negotiated the roads to the higher ground.

It was gratifying, delightful and amusing to see the whole group so excited at being able to throw snowballs at each other, before returning to the vehicle in a buoyant mood; if a little wet.

During the Christmas break, we had problems with a blocked heating system and one of my enduring memories was seeing the entire visiting party huddled around a five-kilowatt log-burner; each wearing two or three borrowed coats over their own clothes, to keep warm in the sub-zero temperatures.

After an enjoyable if rather tiring holiday for everyone, I drove the entire group comprising Don, Valery, Cycil, Sherry, Chief Masipe Matlou and Sharon to Manchester Airport.

On the way, one of the visitors asked if we could make a detour to Manchester United's ground to have a look as two of them were avid supporters. It didn't take long for us to get there and we had plenty of time before their departure, so Don asked if we might be able to get a tour of the ground. I was a little doubtful that we should get in because it was the Sunday before most of the country returned to work and the car park was empty but for a few cars. Nevertheless, with a real dignitary amongst us, there was an improved chance of success.

I entered the building and managed to find a person of authority, who was not only delighted to meet the Zulu Chief but who very kindly gave us an express tour of the site, leaving suitable time for me to get them to their scheduled flight. They even came away with some cherished souvenirs.

Our happy and grateful band of travellers hauled and heaved their possessions, souvenirs and presents to the check-in desks and bade the family farewell with hugs and kisses. As they left the concourse into the security gate, Don embraced me and said:

"Ach, you know Paulus, Chief Masipe Matlou translates into English as Chief Shit-face!"

Chapter Thirty-One

PROCESSED FOOD

INTO THE new spring term and I received an invitation from the headteacher of the local upper school, to deliver a themed assembly of my choice to Year Eleven, comprising a number of our previous pupils. I was happy to do this as it gave me an opportunity to find out how some of them were progressing and Ofsted were always grading levels of 'continuity' and joint responsibility. However, it would have to be good because students of this age do not bear fools or mediocrity gladly. I wasn't going to get away with one of Aesop's fables and a popular primary school song such as 'One More Step Along the World I Go' or 'He's Got the Whole World in His Hands'. So, after some thought and a little preparation, I went to the gig armed with a tin of cat food, a tin-opener and two tablespoons.

After a warm introduction from the Head of Year, I appeared front and centre stage, to be confronted with sullen looks of indifference from both pupils and staff. They all looked like they needed an injection of interest! Holding up the can, I gave them my opening gambit:

"I don't know about you, but I love cat food."

This was greeted with instant, uncomfortable squirms and wriggling, accompanied with tortured and grotesque looks of abhorrence... Great, correct response, I thought. This'll wake 'em up!

"Yep, I just can't get enough of the stuff. It's great on toast, in sandwiches, I even put it in stews."

I was confronted with more exaggerated contemptible looks along with sounds of disapproval and disgust. The Head of Year anticipated what was coming and wondered if I was going to breach health and safety regulations.

"I've got a tin-opener here, would someone like to come down and do the honours?"

An individual stood up, accepted the invitation and came to the front with the gait and manner of someone desperate to call my bluff.

"Here, hold the can, can you confirm to everyone it hasn't been opened?" He nodded his head and confirmed it hadn't been tampered with.

"Good, open it up then."

He dutifully applied the opener and removed the lid.

"I can't wait!" I said, rubbing my hands in mock anticipation. I revelled in the moment and slowly dipped my spoon into the contents to increase the level of tension and anticipation. As I brought the spoon to my lips, the sounds of revulsion rose in volume and I genuinely thought a girl on the front row was going to faint, or at least throw up. The boy who had opened the pet food just stared disbelievingly at me with his mouth open.

"You've got your mouth open; do you want some?" He hastily retreated to his seat, shaking his head both in shock and rejection.

"Hey, don't knock it until you've tried it. Is there anyone here brave enough to have a taste?"

This time the Head of Year removed herself from her seat and came over to me. Looks of horror were etched on the faces of both staff and pupils and the hall erupted into fits of anxiety and consternation. The Head of Year whispered into my ear: "I don't think this is a good idea."

I whispered back: "Don't worry, I know what I'm doing. You can return to your seat. No one's getting poisoned."

As she walked back, other members of staff appeared to voice their disapproval, but she performed a downward gesture of both hands, as if to say sit and quieten down.

"So, who's brave enough to come and have a taste?"

There were plenty of 'Talk to the hand…' gestures and the shaking of heads, but I repeated the invitation. This time peer pressure came into play as some pupils pushed a reluctant 'volunteer' off his seat and persuaded him to take up the challenge. The disinclined individual offered some resistance but realised that the perceived discomfort of the impending ordeal was better to endure rather than the dishonour and disgrace of refusal.

Down to the front he limped with the cries of brutal encouragement resounding in his ears.

"Well done, at least you're brave enough to try. What's your name?" I repeated it as I endorsed his unwilling act of valour. I whispered in his ear… "Trust me."

I plunged the second spoon into the cat food and offered it up to the taut and grimacing face of the individual, who braced himself for an unpleasant experience. As the spoon entered his mouth, the increasing sounds of disgust and mock hysteria from the onlookers – not to mention the genuine concern of the staff – slowly fell away, as his tense facial muscles slowly relaxed to an unexpected taste that appealed to his senses, which in turn confused the disappointed audience.

"Nice?"

"Mmmmm!" came the reply.

"Another?"

"Mmmmm yes please!"

Much to the relief of his surprised teachers and the anticlimactic response of his peers, the pupil returned to his seat, though not to any adulation but, rather, much questioning.

As the excitement subsided, I explained to the receptive students that despite their obvious disappointment the can did not contain cat food. The previous night I had hacksawed a baked bean can in half and emptied out the contents. I refilled the two halves of the can with a mixture of chocolate Angel Delight and diced-up Mars bar. I then soldered the two halves of the can together and wrapped a cat food label around it. The label hid my 'metal-work' and no one was the wiser. Having both ends of the can intact, gave my ruse further credibility. Then came the punchline.

"Most, if not all of you will have heard of the phrase 'judging a book by its cover'. Contrary to popular belief, first impressions don't always count. we often make the wrong judgements based on first impressions. In its very worst form, some of us make morally wrong judgements about the colour of people's skin. We see their 'label' as a means by which indefensible assumptions are drawn. We call it racism! Thank you.

I stood back as the students and staff applauded generously. As they filed out, the Head of Year came over, thanked me for the powerful message and admitted to being entirely fooled by the demonstration.

"I was truly worried," she said.

"It wouldn't have been as powerful or engaging had you known from the beginning."

"No, but it might have prevented me from doubting your intentions. Will you come back?"

"Certainly, a pleasure." And I did and presented a talk on Nelson Mandela and why he was named so, but that is another story. Teaching children tolerance is easy, it's the backdrop of their lives we have little or no influence over. Sometimes irreparable damage has been served on impressionable minds by the time they arrive in school.

Chapter Thirty-Two

PLANNING FOR ALL EVENTUALITIES

AFTER THE Government of the time promoted the growth of Children's Centres the length and breadth of the country, I was invited by the Local Authority to have one built on site. These I felt were a good idea and sat well with my own philosophy of earlier-the-better and life-long learning. The idea was to get parents on-side early and provide social assistance, workshops and home visits; enabling them to give their children a positive start on their educational journey. In effect, the 'Early Years Foundation Stage' would now range from 0-5 years; in my opinion, the most impressionable and influential time in a child's life. This required a multi-agency or faceted approach and the keywords were 'support' and/or 'intervention'. I had a wonderful Centre Manager who had gained relevant and transferable skills working as a Learning Mentor as well as links to Youth-Offending Teams (YOT).

My only proviso in agreeing to having a Children's Centre was that it had to be an integral part of my school and not a standalone building. Along with subsidies received, I knew that my school budget would be 'raided' to a certain extent, to fund this substantial building project, so I wanted 'locked in' building extension benefits if the national initiative went 'tits-up'. In addition, we could allow for plans drawn up to include designs that provided overall symmetrical and aesthetical improvement to our building.

The company appointed to the task had a good Project Manager who oversaw the logistical challenges involving continuity and health and safety issues. The whole undertaking including planning and construction took approximately eighteen months, with minimal disruption considering the enormity of the task and the antagonistic tendencies of my then Site Manager who presented our site visitors with unnecessary and unacceptable resistance.

Thankfully, he was later replaced with an appointed Site Supervisor; an ex-kitchen-fitter who possessed more than a modicum of common sense and the requisite skills, to allow me to step back from the onerous building management issues, to concentrate on teaching. He became a loyal and hardworking confidant.

The finished scheme looked truly remarkable and certainly increased our capacity for delivering excellent educational provision. Our building became a flagship establishment within the authority and my Site Supervisor and Centre Manager played significant roles towards us achieving that status.

We managed to invite veteran broadcaster Harry Gration of BBC *Look North* for its opening ceremony. I was impressed by his kindness and professionalism and he drew a large crowd of onlookers and interested parties.

As well as our Inspire project, the Children's Centre brought in many more parents, who rightly saw it as a means of boosting their own as well as their children's life chances.

I had a fabulous time teaching parents how to prepare

a basic three-course Christmas meal for a family of four, on a budget of only five pounds!

I really welcomed the extended space which perfectly serviced our breakfast club and dining facilities, providing most of our pupils with at least one hot meal each day.

Chapter Thirty-Three

VOICES IN THE MIST

WHEN RYAN came to us, he had been excluded from two other schools. This was not unusual for our school, as we were fast adopting a reputation for accommodating 'challenging' individuals with behaviour or special educational needs (SEN).

My Special Needs Coordinator and I would disbelievingly read or baulk at the reports submitted by previous schools, which revealed much lower levels of tolerance towards these pupils. These children were not only let down quite often by inadequate or negligent parenting, but also by poor thresholds of patience and behaviour management.

What I most liked about Ryan, was his ingenuousness. He couldn't lie and would always 'spill the beans' when quietly questioned and put at ease. He was a solidly built young lad, much bigger in stature than all his year group peers and totally unaware of his own strength. He was short of friends, mostly because they were wary of him and when they didn't let him join in their games, he would lose his temper and end up battering someone. He was easily misled and found himself in all sorts of trouble when other children 'set him up' as it were.

I would often seek Ryan's testimony if he were witness to some misdemeanour, as inevitably he would tell the truth and not have to worry about any repercussions because nobody would confront him about 'grassing them up'. In doing so, I would take the opportunity to reinforce his role as informer by telling other individuals during questioning that I believed Ryan because he didn't make a habit of telling lies. He took this as a 'badge of honour' thus promoting the benefits of sound child psychology.

This refreshing example of honesty made him the subject of one of my poems:

Accused
"Who did that?"
"Miss, it was Jamie miss."
"How can you be so certain Ryan?"
"'Cos it was me and I'm lying."

Ryan was often sent to me as he got older and usually by one member of staff in particular.

This would annoy me for two reasons: firstly, it would disrupt my work and secondly because it showed a lack of professionalism on the part of the teacher concerned.

The following conversation would inevitably ensue:

"Hello Ryan, why have you been sent to me?" (As if I didn't know.)

"I've been sent out for talking."

"What, in a classroom for learning and social inter-action?" (The sarcasm was lost on him, but he nodded anyway.)

"And were you talking?"

"Yes, even though I was told not to and someone laughed when I got sent out, so I pushed him off his chair."

"Was this person hurt?"

"No."

"But that wasn't right was it, you could have hurt them?"

"Yes, but I didn't." (Again an honest and accurate observation.)

"OK, thanks for telling me. You go back to class and work hard and tell your teacher to see me at lunchtime." (Being told to come and see me during her break by the child she had sent out would definitely piss her off, but it was an opportunity to impose upon her valuable time.)

"Yes sir, but my teacher said I had to stay with you."

"Well, that's not possible because I don't have a spare bedroom at home." (Confused look, then the penny dropped.)

"That's funny, sir." (And he smiled so warmly and disarmingly and left.)

His teacher wasn't impressed at all and felt angry and undermined. However, I had very little patience for her inability to come up with a better plan of action than frequently sending him to me, so I questioned her methodology:

"When a child is sent to me, it should be for two reasons: firstly, because you want them to show me good work, in which case you can send them at *any* time, even if I'm engaged in an important meeting. Nothing is more important than a child's success. Secondly, the child in question has committed a heinous act, punishable by exclusion and every conceivable method of control or means of punishment has been exhausted. Is this the case or are you telling me that you cannot cope?"

The final comment provoked a look of rebuff. She rightfully said:

"He's a continual menace who disrupts my lessons and distracts other children."

"Agreed, he also needs some understanding, so why not use some positive encouragement on him? I suggest

236

you find a small element of success with which you might pour a disproportionate amount of praise on him and then send him to me for a good work sticker. All kids love getting stickers. Better still, engineer an outcome that allows you to send him to me for a Headteacher's Gold Award sticker. That will completely wrong-foot him. Prove to him that you *do* have a heart. He doesn't think you do. In return, I'll take him out of your lesson for an hour each week to attend 'Wider Opportunities' music lessons with the year below. He *might* just find an instrument that he likes playing."

Still smarting from my previous comment, she rose from her chair sporting an indignant look and left.

I think her plan of action was to try and send him to me as many times as possible, to try and disrupt my itinerary, but it didn't work because all I was confronted with was a proud grin (he did have a lovely smile) and an opportunity to heap more praise on him.

The following week I entered his music lesson and asked the music teacher how Ryan was coping. He looked at me with a wry grin as if to thank me for this 'unexpected pleasure of disruption' and said:

"Out of all the instruments he could have picked up, he had to choose the trombone, didn't he?"

I smiled:

"Do you think he could get a tune out of it?"

"Well, he's got the right embouchure!"

At that moment, Ryan made his way over to me holding the trombone in a clumsy manner and after making an appeal for me to listen, proceeded to 'rip out' a huge glissando. He followed this up with a wide grin, as if we had just given him a licence to conjure up as much noise as possible.

If anyone were to get a tune out of Ryan, it would be

this teacher. I left Ryan in his capable hands and hoped he would get something of value out of him.

Later during a seasonal concert, when traditionally we would have a number of soloists performing, I was immensely pleased to introduce a very nervous Ryan to front and centre stage, to perform a short exposition of his limited material.

To this day I have never forgotten the look of pride and achievement on his face as the audience erupted into a round of adulation. It was tear-inducing.

That year, our assessments and evaluations revealed that a significant number of boys in Year Six, of which Ryan was included were falling behind. As a result, some 'booster' lessons were necessary to try and redress the balance. So, during the spring term, I agreed to take a group of 'challenging' boys twice a week for a literacy hour. It was fair enough, if I couldn't make any progress with these individuals, how could I criticise or advise anyone else?

However, in order to avoid stigmatizing the individuals, I decided to call the lessons 'Master-class Workshops' and thought very carefully about the content and lesson planning.

Finally, I decided to promote literacy through art and felt that a well-structured approach to art appreciation and description could be applied to so many genres.

I would project a classic artwork onto the whiteboard and encourage the boys to form a 'spidergram' in order to systematically write down various but familiar observations using prompts, such as:

1. Introduction: Is this a landscape, seascape or portrait artwork?
2. Who painted it and in which year?

3. What or who can you see in the picture? Can you think of an imaginary name?
4. What colours are used?
5. How is the paint applied e.g. brush or palette-knife, rough or smooth texture?
6. Talk about the atmosphere created, e.g. sad, happy, bright bleak, sinister, etc.
7. Is there any movement in the painting and how is this produced?
8. Conclusion. What are your feelings?

The first question or prompt would always provide the writer with two or three sentences, without them having to think too hard; thus providing an initial impetus to their work.

As an aid to SEN children, I might give them worksheets with multiple choices.

In any event, the boys became quite adept at this style of appreciation and their results were well received during an Ofsted inspection; so much so that the visiting inspector graded the lesson as 'Excellent' and asked if she could take samples to show other schools. Of course, this generated no small amount of pride for my group but not as much as the occasion when I took some of them to the Yorkshire Show and they had an unexpected chance to show off their skills once more.

I purposely had six of these boys forming my group during the visit to avoid any potential behaviour incidences, but I genuinely enjoyed their company and I found them very responsive to me.

As they walked around the show in uniform for safety reasons, one of them spotted a large marquee with paintings on sale and asked if they could go in to look at them. I agreed to this being a good idea. As we entered, the boys became excited about the cost of the artworks on show;

some of which revealed price tags of multiple thousands. At the same time, a rather pompous-looking owner or manager adorned in a two-piece suit with contrasting waistcoat, stylish watch chain secured to his buttonhole and equally unstylish frayed shirt-cuffs, approached me in a purposeful stride:

"I'm sorry I can't allow these youngsters in here amongst this very expensive fine art."

"Oh, and why not?"

"For obvious reasons, I would have thought, the paintings may get damaged."

"Oh, I don't think so, they really appreciate good art."

"Still, I don't think it's a good idea," he protested in his superior, supercilious, sanctimonious and self-righteous way.

"Hayden," I called.

"Yes, Mr Franklin?"

"Come over here and tell me something about this picture."

"It's very nice, Mr Franklin – a seascape. I can't read the artist's name or say when it was painted, but the scene is a rough sea and the dark colours reveal bad weather and gales. The artist shows movement through high waves and white foam. The texture is thick. I like it but it's a bit scary for the sailors."

The man's bottom lip fell away, and turned to Hayden, revealing the artist's name and the year in which he produced it.

"You're a talented young lad!" he exclaimed.

"Mr Franklin taught us all how to talk about art."

To the man's credit, he turned to me and apologised for being hasty in his judgements. He then generously invited the boys to stay as long as they wanted and invited others to express their observations.

Eventually, I withdrew the boys and rewarded them all with a well-earned ice cream.

It was a very satisfying day and even the report that one of our pupils had gone missing from another group didn't ruin it. Devorah, the group leader was beside herself with grief and guilt, but the boy in question had followed our well-rehearsed 'lost' protocol to the letter and dutifully reported in at the prescribed office. With map in hand, he proudly lauded his orienteering skills and earned himself membership into my after-school walking club; reinforcing my belief that children can be dependable.

I used to love the company of my pupils off-site and by the same token, they had the advantage of getting to know more about my character outside the formal constraints of school. I really think they came round to liking me, though I think they liked the ice-creams more.

It used to break my heart at times, when I would arrive at school early in the morning, to see a lonely, cold and wet Ryan leaning up against the wall outside his class-room; having waited since 7.30 a.m. after his Mother used to drop him off on her way to work. As ever, I would ask him if he had eaten anything. Invariably, the answer would be the same -"No."

I would escort him into the breakfast club, where the kind-hearted coordinator would find something to warm the poor soul up. Frequent requests to his Mother to get him to school later or join the breakfast club fell on deaf ears.

This used to anger me because children should always be your first priority and consideration. Above all, they should never be cold or hungry. I would always feed and clothe children whose parents were genuinely unable to, but it was rare, as most parents would do anything to make sure their primal needs were met.

Many children would come back to see us after their

move to the High School, for a while anyway and Ryan would always be one of them. He was well met.

After my promotion to senior management, I missed the fun of the classroom and my decision to maintain an amount of contact with the children wasn't just to maintain my teaching and judgemental observation credibilities. The children were great company and often made me laugh; not to mention providing the perfect excuse for me not having to become administratively constipated.

The value of laughter in the learning process can never be underestimated and I remember one particular occasion when a girl in Year Six asked me for permission to bring in her giant African snails to show others. Naturally, my Deputy Head rang the 'Klaxon bell' of health and safety, a bandwagon he had leapt upon as 'Children's Safety Officer' and like so many unnecessary times before, tried to dissuade me; this time on the grounds of "the spread of disease". His clarion calls on the banning of snowball fights and conkers, were also ignored. Whilst I agreed to the use of safety glasses with conkers, he would have had combatants in both disciplines dressed like ship-building welders!

Despite his disproportionate appeals of protest, I allowed the young girl to bring in the snails on the understanding that an adult took them away after we had finished using them as a focus of discussion. I wasn't concerned they might evade capture, should they get free, but more mindful of them getting snail-napped.

We used to call this kind of event 'spontaneous teaching' which of course became almost impossible with the lack of digression from prescribed programmes of study and 'teaching to the test'; another Gove gaff.

After an engaging session on habitat, dietary needs and sexual proclivities of these unusual pets, I decided to have some fun with the young owner of these unhurried and lollygagging mobile home hauliers, by treating her to an old joke:

"You know, 'Lucky', I used to race snails."

"Did you, Mr Franklin? That's interesting."

"Yes I did, but they always came last, so I chopped their shells off to make them go faster."

"Oh Mr Franklin, that was cruel, did that not kill them?"

"No it didn't, it just made them more sluggish."

Lucy gave me a long withering look as the class roared with laughter.

"You know Mr Franklin, your jokes don't improve with time."

Sniggering uncontrollably, I had to agree:

"You're right Lucy, have you ever eaten snails?"

"Yeuch! No I haven't. Why, have you?"

"Of course, I don't like fast food." More sniggers and belly laughs ensued.

After the distraction, we completed some great work that lesson; all within a light-hearted and focused atmosphere. This is what the joy of teaching was all about I thought.

Lucy was a girl to whom teaching and learning didn't come easily, a bit like me back in the day, but she always applied herself and left us with praiseworthy grades.

When I met Lucy's Mother, during parents' evening, she informed me that her daughter very much enjoyed coming to school, despite my jokes. It was these 'nuggets' of acknowledgement that I considered to be special moments in my career and you can't easily get them from non-discovery-based rote learning; although it does have a place, especially in the pursuit of 'times-tables'.

Chapter Thirty-Four

THE YETI

WITHOUT DOUBT, one of the funniest moments of my teaching career involved an Irish Wolfhound that managed to find its way onto our playground.

As soon as he had 'clocked it', as ever, my over-reacting Deputy Head came 'Exoceting' his way to me, highlighting the health and safety risks to which the children were exposed and declaring a "Crisis" and "Emergency!"

I had never heard of any long-haired, flapping-eared, lolloping dog of this kind ever behaving like a Pitbull Terrier, but I humoured him and agreed to get the children in from their playtime, in case they got over-excited or knocked over.

When they were all 'safely' indoors, that should have been the end of the matter, but unfortunately my 'capeless' crusader insisted on going out to hitch it to a fence, whilst waiting for someone to come and collect it.

"'Aren't you going out to help him?" my Head of Lower School asked.

"What in this suit?" I replied.

As my Deputy approached the dog, his long grey flapping mullet must have presented itself to the Irish Wolfhound as an irresistible female enticement, for the dog jumped up launching itself at his flailing body, knocking and pinning him to the floor. That was funny enough, but the dog, with testosterone levels running high, decided to start pumping him with intent from the rear.

That certainly did it for me. Laughter rang out amongst the shocked and entertained onlookers. I couldn't draw breath. I was totally incapacitated by my continuous exhalation of air. As I slowly succumbed to the suffocating effect of my breathlessness, I couldn't help thinking that this was going to be a literal manifestation of the phrase "I died laughing".

Eventually, after what seemed an interminable amount of time, I managed to suck in some oxygen and my Deputy struggled to his feet. As he came into the building, bustling through the corridor where I and other colleagues were waiting, he stared forward, wide-open-eyed, sweeping the dishevelled hair from his face, failing to regain any composure. Likewise, neither could I, as I slowly forced my fist into my mouth, failing to halt the emitting whimpering pulses.

I retreated to my office, where I bit on a wooden ruler to try and stop my convulsive laughter. Fighting back tears, I tried unsuccessfully to erase what I had witnessed from my memory. It was useless, a memory-moment had already formed in my head.

And that wasn't all, a small, young girl from Year One recognised the dog as hers (not hard) and went out to it. Standing barely at the same height as the animal, she clasped his collar and walked him over to the fence, where she tied up his trailing lead, until her mother came to collect the daft, canine creature.

Chapter Thirty-Five

RIFTS

THERE WERE constant disagreements throughout my teaching career and to be fair, I certainly welcomed them when they were constructive. Indeed, challenging people on their views, ideas and opinions certainly required a justification of their decision-making and rational thought processes. I resolutely disliked the 'old school' way of thinking that expected staff and children to do whatever the Headteacher said. Pupil Councils and Parent/Teacher Associations (PTA) were often great forums for presenting sound ideas. Many good reforms were premised on the strength of consensus, which in turn meant everyone 'signed up' for the intended outcome and a pool of skillsets helped realise the intended outcome.

I'd like to say that most disagreements were between children, but invariably this wasn't the case. Managing adults can be difficult at times but unless there is a positive means of arbitration, disputes can fester on. One thing is for sure, an arbitrator *must* listen to both sides of an argument, to form a clear picture of events. Luckily, I possessed ears like dustbin lids and realised that often, an impassioned plea or viewpoint, looked completely different after considering all the facts.

On some occasions, I would ask staff involved to go off-site to discuss their differences over a coffee at a local flower nursery and afterwards, bring back some floral adornments for the school corridors. This often worked because the alternative was a long and arduous complaints procedure, which was usually unwarranted or undesired.

On a few occasions, I resorted to the complaints, discipline or competency procedures to actively dismiss unworthy, ill-disciplined or incompetent staff. However, although a necessary recourse of action at times, following the correct procedural routes and protocols is both lengthy and exhausting.

Of course, when dealing with children and parents, the approach is much the same. Seeking a way to resolve an issue over a discussion, was always the preferred modus operandi and I found the offer of a cup of tea, coffee or soft drink to be the perfect way of letting individuals calm down after venting their spleen.

Once I had a post-graduate ring me and ask why she hadn't secured the advertised post. This was quite common and I welcomed the opportunity to help unsuccessful candidates improve their chances with future applications. However, in this case the young lady asked me if it was because she was disabled!

"No, indeed not!" I replied, because that kind of personal information is neither relevant nor accessible to me and that part of the paperwork is retained by the Authority. I followed this up by stating that her application, depicted by only a number, was weak and overshadowed by another candidate who said more about my school than themself. Furthermore, my Deputy Chair of Governors was also disabled and rightly insisted on the correct protocols being observed.

I remember a statement being made by Michael Caine in an interview concerning his filming profession, who said that race, colour, belief or disability are in his opinion totally irrelevant, compared to a person's ability to fulfil the role, or words to that effect. I'm in total agreement.

We had a very strange, unpleasant and disobedient child at Broomsgrove and once again this was the result of an over-attended and indulged individual, by a doting, disagreeable and argumentative mother.

On one unforgettable occasion at a 'PGL' (established by Peter Gordon Lawrence) adventure camp at Hay-On-Wye, this particular pupil for the sake of anonymity we shall call Shayne and a small group of others were receiving a sailing lesson from a qualified instructor. As a result of his dismissive nature to guidance, Shayne fell overboard and hastily clutched the prow before hitting the surface of the water. Honestly, the cries of life-threatening distress could be heard right across the lake as he cried out at the top of his voice: "Help! I can't hold on, save me! Save me!"

All this noise and unnecessary panic, despite the fact he could swim and was wearing the requisite lifejacket.

"Help, help me!"

By now, his theatrical cries of distress were unsettling the other children, but more importantly, his loud pleas for help were drowning out the quiet, calming words of advice from the instructor, who finding his patience deserting him suddenly and explosively shouted:

"Shut up! Shut up! For the last time, stand up! The water is only three feet deep."

As he stood up in the waist-high water, he had to suffer the ignominy of others' howls of laughter ringing in his ears as they sailed by and the safety boat came to 'his rescue'.

On another occasion during an end of term sports day, a friendly local farmer was giving lifts to pupils in a trailer, slowly being pulled along by his tractor.

The trailer had large, low-inflated tyres with a tailgate. Once again, ignoring safety guidelines, Shayne started to stand up and mess about in the trailer and as a result, got thrown overboard as it hit a small grassy mound. The large, soft tyre travelled over his shoe. Almost immediately, Shayne released a surge of distress calls, disproportionate to the 'injury' he had received. I was first on the scene with a first aid kit that I didn't require, but it took minutes to calm down his ridiculous reaction to the event. Furthermore, his mother came racing to the scene crying hysterically and issuing orders and threats to me and a very concerned farmer.

"Call an ambulance now! Now! She insisted.

"It's not necessary, nothing is broken and he's not traumatised," I replied.

"He is making a lot of unnecessary fuss to detract from the fact that his disruptive behaviour has been the cause of this. He's received a short, sharp shock, but is absolutely fine.

Partly out of relief and embarrassment, she then switched her attack from me onto the farmer, promising to bring legal action against him. I then told her that I would defend him as a witness, along with a large number of onlookers, who had witnessed the boy's reckless behaviour.

"You and your girlfriend haven't heard the last of this," she threatened as she led her son off the field, pampering him with words of overindulgence, comfort and attention, but we had!

The reference to Gwynneth was a result of us both debriefing her on her son's unacceptable behaviour at PGL.

On the subject of briefs, I smiled at the thought of his mother not knowing that I had been obliged to wear some of Gwynneth's underwear for a few days at Hay-On-Wye, because my entire luggage had been left inadvertently on the playground in a small, leather 'Paddington'-like suitcase, as the coach pulled out of the school. Will in his infinite wisdom, had then forwarded it on to me by second-class post, rather than courier to save money. It consequently arrived at PGL as we were leaving to come home. Nevertheless, I was pleasantly surprised to find out just how comfortable they were!

At Downton Primary, we had only several black children on our roll as one might expect in a northern, white-dominated, militant, ex-mining community. Nevertheless, the school was fiercely inclusive, with equality high up the list of priorities.

Towards the end of my incumbency, it became a legal requirement to record and report all racially motivated incidences to a centrally controlled Government website.

One day Jadyn, a young black lad approached me with a complaint, concerning the fact that Ryan had called him a name. My heart immediately sank as I thought the worst. Nevertheless, the investigation of this matter would be easy, because Ryan couldn't help but tell the truth.

I asked Jadyn to sit in my office with the door open and went to find Ryan to get to the bottom of this issue. I escorted him back to where Jadyn was waiting and sat them together.

"Now Ryan, I expect you know why I've brought you here. Jadyn tells me you've been calling him names, is that correct?"

"Yes, Mr Franklin." Good old Ryan, I thought: a prosecuting counsel's dream and a defending lawyer's nightmare.

"Well, what did you say?" (expecting the worst and anticipating mountains of administrative paperwork; not to mention bringing the school's reputation into disrepute).

"I called him fatso, Mr Franklin."

"Well, you know I've got to report this incident to the Government Ryan", not fully internalising his answer and responding on impulse. Ryan nodded.

"Wait a minute, *fatso*?! He's not fat! Why did you call him that?" (imagining my fist-pumping the air).

"I couldn't think of anything else to say."

"Good old Ryan", I thought to myself, "You're not so bad, are you?

"I'm very cross Ryan and you've clearly hurt Jadyn's feelings. I want you to apologise to him."

(Ryan nods as one corner of his mouth turns up in agreement.) "Sorry, Jadyn."

"You know, Ryan, I'm wondering what the great Mahatma Gandhi would have done in a situation such as this?"

"What would he have done, Mr Franklin?" His question belying the fact that he had no idea who Gandhi was.

"Well, I'm sure if he was sat in this seat now talking to you, he would say I would like you to sit next to Jadyn in class for the next week and make friends with him."

"That's a good idea isn't it, Jadyn," said Ryan as a broad smile adorned his face. "I'd like that."

Jadyn looked at me, wondering how my decision had benefitted him and whether justice had truly been served. He nervously gulped as the corner of his mouth turned down and nodded slowly in agreement to Ryan's question.

They got on famously.

Chapter Thirty-Six

BLIZZARD!

OFSTED RETURNED in December 2010 and it couldn't have been more mistimed. By now the protocol for visits had changed and schools received only one-or-two days' notice with smaller assigned teams arriving and departing within forty-eight to seventy-two hours.

When I took the call, a very imperious, supercilious Lead Inspector speedily outlined the pre-determined itinerary; including, of course, examination data retrieved from the Government database.

I discussed with him of course the possible disruption of the poor weather forecast and requested a delay, to which he responded with an emphatic 'No!' as his team were arriving that night at the hotel just a couple of miles from the school. *So, they were OK then.*

After, a late attendance at school the staff and myself left at approximately nine-o-clock.

I requested that my Site-Supervisor call me at five-o-clock the following morning to brief me on the conditions. This he reliably did, and after a sleepless night, I discussed with him, the situation regarding staff travelling safely to the site. Already at my end, fast-growing snow drifts had made my departure impossible. At school, conditions were already worsening and I was not prepared to risk the safety of staff attempting to negotiate the dangerous driving conditions.

I asked that school closure signs be erected until local staff could arrive to issue the closure on our website and Facebook page. I then initiated the school closure protocol and dutifully rang the Lead Inspector at five-thirty. A half comatose official answered his mobile and after establishing who the call was from, proceeded to ask me why I had called him:

"I'm taking the decision to close the school because of the conditions."

"Are you sure?" came the reply.

"*Are you sure*?" I thought. "Yes, it's impossible for me and a majority of my staff to get there and the teacher/pupil ratios would be compromised.

"I see, this is most irregular. I shall have to inform my superiors. Call me first thing tomorrow, my team can carry out some preliminary work today."

The following morning had shown no respite in the weather and I informed the lead Inspector of my intention to keep the school closed:

"Well, we've decided to come anyway."

"The conditions are too treacherous for me to set off just now. The gritters will probably come around again, but not yet," I stated.

"Do you have any staff living locally to the school?" he enquired.

"Yes, my Head of Upper School and two members of the office staff."

"Good, get them to arrive as early as possible. We can get there and we will hopefully see you later."

"*You can get there*!" I thought... "What about the absence of children?" I asked.

"Yes, that's quite irregular and might invalidate the inspection, but I'll ask my superiors if we should proceed, given the extenuating circumstances, so as not to disrupt our schedules. We may still have to postpone the entire inspection anyway."

"Oh good," I thought... "I'll still be risking my life getting to school only to find my foolhardiness a complete waste of time."

I showered and got appropriately dressed and prepared for the weather with a hot drink, food, blanket, grit and shovel. This would be the first time I would go into a conference with an Ofsted Inspection team dressed like Shackleton...if I got there!

Gwynneth told me not to go, but I convinced her that I couldn't leave a skeleton crew to tackle the Ofsted pack alone.

At seven-o-clock, I very tentatively started up the car and gingerly reversed onto the ungritted hill. As I selected first gear, I felt the cold chill of impending disaster, grip my body as the car failed to respond to my actions and slowly started to answer to the laws of physics and gravity. What started as a slow slide on the slippery snow and ice, eventually gathered impetus into an uncontrollable sailing sensation of fear and terror, as the car hurtled down the slope, eventually, but predictably ending up at a forty-five-degree angle in a snow-filled ditch!

"Fuck, fuckity-fuck!" I screamed at the top of my voice, punching the steering wheel and cursing the Lead Inspector. "Now what?"

For a few minutes, I contemplated my position; not angularly but rather my options.

A farm was situated nearby and I appealed to the farmer to tow me out of my predicament. He looked at me in a confused way and started to grin before asking me why I should be so reckless in attempting to drive in these adverse conditions. He didn't use the word 'adverse'.

He called me 'An idiot', a designation I had justly

earned, but within minutes he had successfully extracted me from my embarrassment.

"Nah then lad, ay 'ope thee 'ave th' sense t'get thyself 'ome."

I didn't and thanking him profusely, continued on my quest.

The conditions were appalling and deteriorating by the minute. As I got onto the Barnsley Road I passed a fire engine with one of the crew frantically waving and crossing his hands in an attempt to turn me back. Sound advice but Ofsted were in my school!

After a lengthy journey of many minor mishaps and the constant threat of an impending major one, I eventually turned into the school car park *four hours* later! I was impressed by my Site-Manager's heroic endeavours to clear spaces and paths, although less so by the array of four-wheel-drive BMW SUV motors lined up in echelon.

"So that's why they found it so bloody easy to get here!" I thought.

As I entered the building, it was clear by the look on the faces of my staff, who had walked there, that they had already endured a challenging encounter with the inspectors. My Head of Upper School raised her eyes. I gave her a fleeting look of appreciation with a wink and had barely removed my jacket before a trap-door spider-like Lead Inspector had sunk his teeth into me.

"Thought you wouldn't get her at all, Mr Franklin," he intimated in a self-satisfied way.

"I would have got here a lot sooner in one of those impressive vehicles outside. I've clearly taken a wrong turn in my professional career."

Accepting the 'compliment' of his vehicular superiority, he got straight down to business, with what appeared to be a never-ending carousel of questions relating to 'the data'; the usual *modus operandi* of most Ofsted Inspectors, existing in a bubble of impersonal information and mathematical algorithms. Undeterred, and a veritable veteran of past 'Inspector interrogations', I managed to grab myself a tea, before being invited into my own office by an officious woman wanting to ask me questions on our local, national and international connections. After what had gone before on budgetary and assessment analysis, I welcomed this less intensive though nonetheless important conversation and replied avidly and keenly to her questions. I gave a detailed account of our pyramid school and business ventures, which were a source of impressive funding and pooled initiatives, as well as our continued overseas partnerships.

During this exchange, she suddenly stopped proceedings and said:

"Some good answers, Mr Franklin, but I wish you wouldn't keep referring to that clipboard as a crib sheet for replies to my questions."

Fighting back an overwhelming urge to voice my displeasure, I slowly raised and turned the clipboard towards her, revealing a blank sheet of paper, to her astonishment.

"I've got this in my hand waiting to record anything significant that you may have to say."

At once, she leapt up, simultaneously spouting 'Excellent' as she opened the door to leave.

Soon after, The Lead Inspector announced his decision to award the school an overall grade of 'Good' with 'Excellent' features in Management, Special Needs, Building and Partnerships.

I confess, this is the only inspection I know of, not to have had children resident.

After the 'ordeal' and to our relief, 'We few, we happy few...' locked up and left the premises. I was the last to leave and although my car struggled to free itself from a snowdrift that had emerged on our driveway, I eventually managed to get back to my village in three hours; as far as the pub at the top of our road, where I left the car rather than risk the final downward part of my journey. I celebrated with a pint at the bar where I met a cricketing friend. As we chatted, it suddenly dawned on us both, that it was I who earlier that day he had tried to turn back on the Barnsley Road and he was the firefighter I saw frantically waving his hands:

"We thought, who's this nutter driving in these conditions? Fair play to you and your sense of conviction and duty mate. Have another pint on me."

"Don't mind if I do."

"You're still a nutter, though!"

"Yeah!"

Chapter Thirty-Seven

WAITING FOR A WINDOW

A FEW days later, my family were getting ready to leave for a two-week break over the Christmas holidays in South Africa. We were due to fly from Manchester to Frankfurt for the connecting flight and there didn't seem to be a break in the wintery conditions. It was snowing when we finally took off and by the time we reached Germany, all outgoing flights had been cancelled. We were dreadfully disappointed as the delay meant we would miss Don's birthday. We were put up in a comfortable hotel, but one night's delay turned into two and there were further problems getting on to the long-haul flight, which eventually cost us three days of our first week; and that wasn't the end of it!

After a sapping ten-hour flight, we were delayed at Johannesburg for two hours because our luggage had been lost in transit. We were then advised to return to the airport the following day for any developments.

It was early in the morning and Don set off to drive us back to his house along with the welcoming party. As we joined the motorway, Don was aware of a police car following us.

"Ach! They'll want t' know why there is a large mixed crrrowd travelling this early in the morning and drrrinking beer Paulus."

"But you're not whilst you're driving, Don," I said.

"Ach, it makes no differrrence Paulus. None of your joking Paulus, they have no sense of humourrr."

Two policemen pulled us over and ordered everyone out of the van. In a strong Afrikaans accent and with a lack of respect, he asked for names and the nature of our journey. I couldn't help myself:

"The nature of our journey has been one of delays, disappointment and ineptitude."

"Ach Paulus, don't annoy him," Don whispered out the side of his mouth.

"You're drrrinking," the officer said as he pushed me over the bonnet and searched me, much to the shock of an onlooking Gwynneth.

"Yes, I am, the driver isn't. Why have you pulled us over?"

"*Paulus!*" Don hissed... but I was truly tired and monumentally pissed off.

"Wherrre are you frrrom?" the policeman enquired.

"We've just arrived into the country from England. We are visiting English tourists."

"If this is trrrue, then wherrre is yourrr luggage?"

"You've got me there, some incompetent baggage handler has lost it."

"Passports!" he demanded in a threatening way and in doing so frightened the children.

"Well, you've just taken mine from my pocket!"

Satisfied that we were who we said we were, he again asked about the missing luggage. We explained that we had to come back to the airport the following day, much to our annoyance and gave a forwarding address. Eventually, after more unfriendly interrogation, they let us go.

"Ach Paulus! They'rrre not nice people."

The following day we returned to the airport only to be further delayed and disappointed. So, I made the decision to buy enough clothing for our stay and get on with the business of enjoying ourselves, which frankly, hadn't been possible up to that point.

Having missed Don's birthday celebrations and a planned trip to a leopard sanctuary, we loaded up the van for a trip down to the 'Wilderness', where Don and Valery had rented a lodge for Christmas. The scenery was as beautiful as it was breathtaking and we enjoyed part of Christmas day on the beach; a departure from our usual wintery celebrations at home.

I have great memory-moments of Laura and Gwynneth dressed in African summer-wear and Harry playing cricket with Don on the sand.

In the afternoon, the whole group thoroughly enjoyed a seven-course, three-Michelin-star-like meal for not much more than it would have cost us for a Nando-feast at home.

"Ach! Paulus, yourrre Pound is so strrrong against our weak Rand."

"Well then, let's make the most of it my Broerrr."

After Christmas, we made our way down to Cape Town to celebrate the New Year. We were fortunate that Cycil was able to book student accommodation for a few days. In the reception area, I caught a glimpse of a potted, perfunctorily adorned, single-stemmed, tired and thirsty-looking twig, offering a rather tokenistic gesture of seasonal greeting, but passing as an appropriate salutation to the first four days of our holiday. It's funny how certain details are captured in one's mind.

After an impressive firework display on New Year's Eve, we watched the annual 'Kaapse Klopse' minstrel festival, which is also known as 'Tweede Nuwe Jaar'. At this event we saw literally thousands of minstrels take to the streets in brightly coloured costumes, carrying colourful umbrellas or playing a multitude of musical instruments.

This parade took hours to pass and was truly a carnival of cultural celebration.

Disappointingly, for the second time we were unable to take the cable car to the top of Table Mountain as it had been closed for technical reasons. Nevertheless, we made good of our remaining time together and it was just prior to our departure, that I purchased my prized Christmas tree fashioned out of an Amstel beer can, that still has pride of place on our windowsill every December. It cost me fifty pence but is priceless to me and a testament to the poverty-driven sculpturing skills that can be seen across this beautiful but afflicted country.

At the check-in desk, we were reunited with our lost luggage and to our utter amazement were told that we would have to pay a surcharge for exceeding the baggage allowance.

Rather than accept this as a final indignation, I demanded to see a supervisor who graciously understood our predicament and waived the fee.

As we sat back into our seats after take-off, an announcement came over the speaker from the Pilot. He acknowledged the fact that many visitors had been disappointed by not being able to ride to the top of Table Mountain. As a gesture of goodwill, he had sought permission to deviate from his flight path to fly over it. What a guy! After nonchalantly informing us of his intention, he gently manoeuvred the huge aircraft over, to give everyone a bird's eye view of this magnificent landmark. As a reluctant flyer, I felt comforted by his calm and generous nature, which very much reminded me of Martin Butcher.

To be frank, I never went near the popular seaside resorts frequented by my pupils' families, purely and simply because I always felt on duty and obliged to 'talk shop' or become engaged in earnest conversation with 'concerned' or similarly angry parents, with complaints founded on biased testimonies.

During one summer vacation, my family arrived back at Harwich by ferry after an enjoyable cycling holiday in Holland. I decided to take the more scenic option of our journey back by driving up the east coast. By the time we had wended our way up to Skegness, we were all feeling peckish and ready for refreshment. I parked the car on the front and found a suitable hotel restaurant, with window seating facing onto the shore. We ordered typical fish-fare and appreciatively got stuck into our meal. At some point during our victuals, we were rudely interrupted by a loud and continuous banging on the window, accompanied by raised, excitable chatter.

One of my pupils walking by had recognised me behind the panoramic window and decided to invite his rather large extended family to come over and peer at me, as if I had been a Victorian circus side-show exhibit!

"Look everyone, it's Mr Franklin, Mum, Dad, look it's my Headteacher. (*Bang, bang, aggressively on the window*) Hi Mr Franklin, it's me, William!"

William had pushed his face hard against the glass, crushing his nose and lips into a hideously distorted and twisted fashion, forcing them to appear at mutual angles. Condensation appeared on the colder surface and had started to dribble down the crystal-clear pane. He didn't look that attractive at the best of times but had somehow transformed his more agreeable features into a frighten-ing pose. His persistent distraction was turning our former tranquillity into an uncomfortable period of embarrass-ment. The whole experience left me wondering if all pupils thought I hibernated in a coffin during the school holidays. We didn't see any more of Skegness that day but ended up sprinting like '24 Hours of Le Mans' drivers to the more settling confines of the car and a quick getaway.

Chapter Thirty-Eight

BASIC RULES OF SUCCESS

I THOROUGHLY enjoyed teaching poetry to the upper juniors because I found verse an effective way of improving their descriptive skills when writing prose or examination work. I found that children regarded the demands of poetry to be less onerous than story-writing but appreciated that the rules of success lay in sound planning of subject matter and the correct choice of descriptive words.

I would start with the teaching of Haikus, which allowed the children to work within comforting constraints and didn't overface or intimidate them. I would start by asking individuals or pairs to think of a subject matter – seasons always offered an abundance of options – and then write down descriptive words which best defined their theme. Finally, these choices were governed by limiting syllables.

The next stage was to introduce extended poetry which resulted from the challenge and at times difficulty, in expressing descriptions, emotions and concepts in only three lines.

Once the barriers of choice, flow and rhythm are overcome, then comes the inevitable question – 'Does it have to rhyme?'

I don't recall how many times I've been asked that question but invariably each year I was, but I once responded with a poem I compiled in moments:

Does It Have To Rhyme?
"I've written a poem for you
You can read it if you like."
"I am
But doesn't it have to rhyme?"
"No, not all the time
It can do
Just for you
If you want it to
But then again
It might not –
So there!"

Another question I was always asked in class was:

"How long should my poem be?"

"Any length you wish it to be. Apart from poems with defined restrictions, such as Haikus and Limericks, there are no rules...fill your boots!"

This prompted me in one lesson to inform the children of the shortest poem in the world called 'Ode to a Goldfish' which simply reads as... 'Oh Wet Pet'.

As a result of sharing this with the children, I decided to try my hand at writing an equally short poem, with the humorous addition of a title that was much longer than the content:

Ode to an Obese Feline Quadruped...
(you know where I'm going with this)
'Oh Fat Cat'

The kids loved this, which in turn challenged me to think of an even longer title for a poem of the same length:

Ode to an Ageing Obese Mouse-like Nocturnal Flying Mammal
'Old Fat Bat'

Still on the subject of animals, during one lesson I invited my class to write a poem about their actual or imaginary pets. As usual, I offered to write an example within the time restrictions of the lesson. After the hilarious escapades of the Irish wolfhound and my own experiences of Harley – the beloved miniature Labradoodle of my close friends Clive and Siobhan – I decided to write a poem about dogs. Talking of my 'experiences', I remember turning up at their house one day in a newly purchased pair of 'Crocs'; not the most elegant type of footwear, I agree. Like Marmite, you either love them or loathe them. I think Harley loved them because no sooner had I taken them off, he took off with one of them and returned it later, autographed with a bite-hole surrounded by teeth marks. On another occasion, whilst running eagerly if not maniacally for and returning with a ball that I had been throwing, he suddenly leapt off a nearby stair and landed full square on my lap. The resulting shock of my 'crown jewels' being assailed by his athleticism, immediately forced my body into a painful spatchcocked spasm!

So, 'Dogs' was the theme and to say I have an affinity with dogs is like saying Michael Gove is a close friend of mine. I have no idea why, but for some reason dogs like to use my nether regions as a homing device. Nevertheless, this following poem includes repetition, which is effective in encouraging younger children's involvement:

Dogs Are Great

Dogs are great
A man's best friend
Loyal
Obedient
Company
Sometimes hard-working
We have to take them for walks
Often
They eat a lot
They cost a lot
Vet fees
They chew things
Mostly mine
They scratch things
Mostly mine
And themselves
When they've got ticks
They dig up the garden
And bury things
Mostly mine
They foul the garden
Mostly mine
I clean it up though
Mostly
They growl
They bark
They sniff
And bite
Things...
Mostly mine
Dogs are great
Aren't they?

I always preferred testing my poems on children, as I believed they were the best judges of my style of writing. If they laughed, they were guaranteed funny, if they were moved to express an emotion, then the writing was powerful and accessible. They were always honest enough to say when they didn't understand or like one and if that was the case, it was out.

I once read a book called *Testament of Youth* by Vera Britton – the mother of the late Dame Shirley Williams. It's a tomb. If you attempt to read it, have a dictionary at hand... she must have done. More importantly, though, it is a book about loss and suffering, brought about by the truth and horror of the Great War. Britton claims that her terrible experiences... 'fired her writing to a height of articulateness'.

I consistently observed the traditional two minutes' silence on 'Remembrance Day' with schools throughout my career; not only to emphasise generally, how fortunate our generations had become, but also to mourn ex-pupils whose families had lost serving relatives. I was proud and impressed by the way our children accommodated and recognised the importance of this annual ceremony and the British Legion relied on members of my staff and pupils to support their organised marches with readings and music.

Initially, on earlier 'Remembrance' ceremonies we had to endure the cacophonous, unpleasing, and disharmonious efforts of a bravely willing, though incompetent bugle player. The 'Last Post' became the 'last straw'. Honestly, Ryan could have done so much better on his first attempt at playing the trombone. To be fair, standing there in the cold and often wet conditions, waiting for this onslaught on the ears, it reminded me of the 1960s TV series *F Troop* when an unfortunate, bumbling, bugle-player receives an Indian arrow up the bell of his instrument.

Eventually, I managed to persuade the organisers and my music teacher that the latter should perform the task annually, which he very kindly and professionally undertook.

Britton's book inspired me to write and use the following poem as a reading, but more importantly as a teaching tool for my older pupils. I even used it when teaching my 'challenged' boys group and do you know what?... apart from one or two words that needed to be defined, they really got it. So, like the other accepted ones, it went for publication:

The Death of Reason
(A remembrance Poem)

With pounding heart
Heaving breast and panting lung
He runs
For death beckons and awaits
His or others' life
It matters not
Inexorably the moment comes
Irreversibly irretrievably
The moment arrives
The cold Earth receives her son
Littered and strewn with torn flesh
And stained with life's blood
All joy all youth hope and reason
Are crushed gone lost – forever

Lest we forget.

Chapter Thirty-Nine

ALTITUDE SICKNESS

I HAD a warning in the spring of 2011; not the verbal or written type, but a health one and I didn't ignore it.

I awoke one Friday morning with a tightening pain in my chest and being of an age regarded by many as a time of vulnerability, decided to have it checked out.

I approached my wife to share my concerns and with the compassion and warmth of a loving spouse, she said:

"Well, you'd better get yourself off to the doctors, then."

"I was rather hoping you might take me," I appealed.

"Can't, I'm teaching."

So, off I drove to the doctors with enough work to occupy me whilst waiting… *as you do*!

To be honest, this wasn't the only time Gwynneth had refused to accompany me to the Doctors or hospital and I can't help thinking it was because I married her out of badness because of the 'scissors incident'.

During the previous summer, I had been playing cricket and being conscious of injury, wore a helmet during a fast bowler's spell. When I had been fortunate enough to see him off and a spinner came into the attack, I rather stupidly took my 'lid' off.

This slow delivery came towards me and I hurled my

bat at the ball, only to top-edge it and smash it into my face; thus forcing my incisors through my bottom lip!

The umpire advised me to retire (as if he needed to) and I left to walk the short distance home. On the way, I met Gwynneth coming the other way with the kids on bikes.

"I've just split my lip love and need to go to the hospital." (I shouldn't have needed to explain, as my whites were covered in red.) "Can you drive me to the hospital?"

"No, we're just going on a bike ride."

So, I took my leave and drove to the hospital nine miles away, with my mouth tightly shut to stem the bleeding. I made my way to Accident and Emergency and was seen quite quickly by the triage nurse who said I would be seen presently. And I was, *two hours later*, during which time I saw other patients jump the queue, having arrived after me. One of these was a rather obese-looking youngster, who had been brought in by his over-reactive parents on account of suspected earache. It hadn't occurred to them to seek advice from a chemist or dial 111. Oh no, this necessitated a trip to A and E where they plonked him down on one of the chairs and he happily munched his way through two 'Grab-Bag'-sized packets of crisps, washed down by a litre of orangeade, without exhibiting signs of any distress; well apart from some whinging about running out of sustenance. As they took him in before me, I feebly, tried to voice some coherent words of complaint through my tightly bonded lips, whereupon the nurse said:

"It's because of our child priority policy."

"Does your 'death-by-eating' policy override your 'bleeding-to-death' policy, I mumbled pitifully and incoherently.

Adding insult to injury, when I was eventually seen by a doctor, he announced that there was nothing he could do and so advised me to go home and continue to keep my mouth tightly shut until the bleeding stopped. What a waste of 'bleeding' time! Although, to be fair, mouth injuries do heal quickly and by the time I got back, the game was still in progress, so I fielded with my mouth shut throughout. I couldn't even appeal when I thought players were out!

Anyway, having driven myself to the local doctors' surgery, this time I was seen with a little more urgency, which conversely unsettled me.

"I don't think you are having a heart attack, Paul, but your symptoms would suggest otherwise, so I'm going to give you a tablet to widen the arteries, which will give you a bit of a headache and then I'm going to call an ambulance to be on the safe side."

And so, within minutes, I was 'blued and twoed' on my way to Huddersfield Infirmary, sitting in a chair with a banging headache, which was worse than the minor chest pain, wondering who was taking the assembly that morning.

As we were speeding along, the noise of the siren made me think of the last time I was in an ambulance with Laura and Harry, a few years before. I had taken the kids to the local driving range before collecting a brand new Audi. Harry had played golf before, but Laura was a total novice. Harry was left-handed and Laura right-handed, so for safety reasons, I positioned them on the far sides of their individual bays, rather than just opposite each other. Just as Harry took an almighty swing with a driver, Laura came across her bay to see the shot. She saw it all right, it connected with her left eyebrow and opened up a sizeable gash. What is it with eyebrow wounds that bleed so profusely? I laid Laura down and applied pressure to the fissure as I shouted for help. It eventually came in the guise of a twenty-something assistant with an alarming look of vacancy:

"Please get me a first-aid box quickly."

"I don't know where it's kept," was his pathetic response.

"What? Well go and look then, you should bloody-well know."

He came back moments later… "No."

"No what?"

"No, I can't find one."

"Well do you have a freezer?"

"Yes, but I'm not allowed to use it."

"Get some frozen package and bring it to me, then call for a fucking ambulance. Do you know the number, it begins with a 9!?"

Another golfer accompanied him to the kitchen, so the idiot didn't get lost and called the emergency services on his mobile. He managed to find a bag of peas that I wrapped into my fleece and applied it to Laura's face.

The ambulance was on the scene in minutes and we all travelled to the hospital in it. Steve, the driver kept Harry occupied by letting him sound the siren. I wanted a go!

Harry then turned to me and said, in his own inimitable way:

"Dad, will I be under-arrested?"

"No, you won't be arrested Son, but your Mother will be when she murders me!"

Laura was eventually sewn up and luckily, with the line of the scar beneath her eyebrow.

She was very brave and undemanding, unlike the child that had queue-hopped when I busted my lip.

Naturally, I was late picking up the new car and although Laura was excited by the new 'wheels' which she tried to 'sell' enthusiastically to Gwynneth, the latter was having none of it.

As I drove worryingly to the same hospital but feeling like a fraud as cars veered over to allow passage of the siren-emitting ambulance, I couldn't help but think the golfing incident may have been the reason for Gwynneth leaving me to arrange my own subsequent hospital admittances. I couldn't think for long, as my head was banging, like it was being bounced by a basketball player.

When we got to A and E, I was placed in a chair where I remained for *several hours*!

After what seemed, and was, an age, a young lady approached me with an E.E.C. machine.

"Have you any pain in your chest now?"

"No", I replied.

"Errm, can't see anything unusual on the screen, but we'll give you a CT scan in a short while."

I was transferred to a bed, where for the next couple of hours, I observed members of staff swap chit-chat and giggles and peruse x-rays studiously. Eventually, a CT scan was rigged up to me and again showed no sign of disorder.

The nurse said kindly but dismissively that she couldn't find anything wrong, so then informed me that I was to be discharged. Having discussed the very real chest pain ordeal and enquired if there were any other tests that might be carried out before receiving negative responses, I meekly asked if I could have something to eat.

"Haven't you had anything? I'll get you something."

She then brought me a large cheese sandwich with lashings of mayonnaise and after expressing my bewilderment, thanks and gratitude, I drove to school where I remained catching up on my in-tray into the night.

Chapter Forty

SHORT REST, RECUPERATION AND REFRESHMENT

IN OCTOBER 2012 Clive, not Olive invited me and Harry to his townhouse in Portugal with his son Rory for a week of golf during half-term. When I first saw this property several years before during a summer break, I was extremely glad of the rest and recuperation it afforded us, after such a busy and stressful school year. Entering the lounge area, one is immediately presented with a backdrop of Atlantic Ocean azure and a long sandy beach, disappearing into the distance, through panoramic windows. On waking up in the morning, nature provides its own alarm call with the sound of waves gently breaking on the shoreline and gulls chattering and squabbling above. The act of lying back and listening is priceless therapy.

The nearest golf club is Praia Del Rey a remarkably beautiful links course and expensive to play. We only booked the single day, so I had enough remaining cash to eat!

We landed on the Saturday and after availing ourselves of the golf range facilities on the Sunday morning, decided to go to a familiar restaurant for lunch. We had all been to this place before at night and agreed that the food and service were second to none. However, we had not visited it on a Sunday lunchtime before and were not expecting to dine fancifully.

When we sat down, the owner came to take our orders. She informed us that Sunday lunchtime was when locals came to partake in traditional dining, but we could order a la carte.

"Absolutely not," I said. Why put the chef to more bother when we can eat the food of the residents."

"Are you sure?" Said the owner. "You may not be familiar with its presentation or content."

" Yes, we're sure aren't we? It would be enjoyable to engage with the townsfolk."

So, that was agreed and we sat back with our drinks and waited. I knew Harry was Hungry and the rest of us were definitely peckish.

The food was delivered in a stew-pot. At first glance, it presented itself as a traditional peasant meal. It certainly was not fine dining, comprising boiled whole leaf and stem cabbage, some kind of boiled orange (obviously paprika or cinnamon-filled) sausage, which visibly glowed like some irradiated Chernobyl butcher's meat and pork joint, complete with a veritable rug of hairs.

"Get stuck in then, boys," I uttered encouragingly, knowing that if it tasted like it looked, we might have problems; less so with Harry, I thought, as he would thrash anything down.

Clive and I continued to talk as the boys less-than-feverishly adorned their plates with the basic fare.

After a short while, I was conscious of no eating going on. It was obvious to me that Rory had declined to participate but Harry was showing signs of being fussy, a characteristic that did not sit well with my misguided philosophy on food.

"Come on Harry, it's not that bad and if the chef has

gone to the trouble of cooking it, the least you can do is honour the time it has taken to prepare."

"Time and trouble," I thought to myself; the chef has just thrown water over this one-pot wonder and gone off for a siesta.

"I can't eat it, Dad – sorry, it's awful." Rory chimed in with some choice nouns and adjectives, finally plumping for 'the orange sausage of doom' – a reasonable and pretty accurate description.

"Harry!" I shouted from my moral high ground (I have been guilty of giving him a hard time on occasions) There are children going hungry all over the world and would be only too pleased to eat this."

"Then let them have it, Dad. It's awful, you try it."

I took a large portion of the dish-of-the-day and set about eating it. I wouldn't be wrong in describing the fibrous and chewy cabbage as having the same smell, colour, texture and taste of an old micro-cloth, that has been discovered weeks after its use, stuffed into a utility-room cupboard. No self-respecting death-row inmate would choose this option as a final meal, although it could have quite conceivably constituted someone's final meal. I'm sure it would take years of conditioning to convince any local child that this was a preferred national dish; much longer to persuade them that it contained any possibility of nutritional value.

We all sat about hungrily mourning the passing of this dish, until the owner came over and enquired as to why we had left so much.

"Was it not to your taste?" she said.

"No, it's lovely," I lied. We're just not that hungry."

"Oh dear, never mind," she said, "I'll put it in a doggy bag for you to take away."

"Please don't," I said to myself... "Oh thank you," were the words that came out.

We vacated our seats and took our leave with the toxic waste. As we left, I couldn't help but notice how the locals were chomping and slurping their way through this offering and wondered how on earth someone had unified these noxious ingredients into some kind of recipe.

We found a suitable receptacle on the way back and deposited the offensive package. We immediately drove straight on and wouldn't have been surprised to learn that the owner of the bin had called out their version of the Health and Safety Executive.

We found a takeaway and went to see the release of the latest Bond film, *Skyfall*.

For the rest of that evening, I suffered an earworm of Adele's unique and dulcet tones reciting the title music:

"Skyfooo let it crumbooo…"

I repeated the tune as if it were on a loop, complete with exaggerated, strangled voice trills.

Harry and Rory suggested eating the 'orange sausage of doom' would have been preferable.

Chapter Forty-One

BACK TO EARTH
WITH A BUMP

BY THE time Autumn 2013 came about, I was having serious difficulty breathing through my nose because of a degenerating condition of acute rhinitis. I had completely lost all sense of taste and smell and my incessant coughing was beginning to worry staff. Embarrassingly, I was continually having to leave meetings and assemblies in mid-flow and I was also suffering a recurrence of my chest pains. By the time Ofsted appeared on our premises around Christmas time, I was genuinely exhausted, worried and a little bit frightened. In short, 'I hit the wall'.

I was ready to resign my post but followed the advice of my Chair and Deputy Chair of Governors, who suggested I go on long-term sick leave to consider my options.

Stupidly, at first, I was reluctant to ruin my attendance record, but close and kind friends persuaded me to make the sensible decision.

I took the full allocation of leave to recuperate, receiving excellent support from Governors, Union representatives, my doctor and occupational health services. I eventually made the decision to retire from teaching and was humbled by the messages of regret and thanks from my staff; many of whom hired a coach to come to my hometown to say goodbye at a concert at the local cinema venue.

So that was it. I decided to occupy myself with voluntary work at my cricket club and a tree-planting charity for the interment of deceased person's ashes. Both provided me with the benefits of outside and environmental work.

Frequently, I would sit down with the relatives of the deceased and happily provide the time to hear them talk about their loved ones. It was comforting for them to have me afford the time to listen. I became acutely aware of the value this service and the healing qualities of the environment and nature. I took time to recognise and watch wildlife, whilst providing habitats for them. The outdoor work was rewarding. I could readily identify trees by their bark, fruit or leaves, depending on the time of year.

The groundsman work at my local cricket club was less rewarding and probably more stress-inducing. I would sit on old and worn-out machinery for up to four hours, three times a week, cutting the outfield. I would travel in ever-decreasing circles on clapped-out mowers as the blunt blades chewed, rather than cleanly cut the blades of grass. It would have been more efficient letting hordes of sheep or masticating cows tear at the ground, if it were not for the fact that they would have buried the outfield in shit!

As I travelled round the boundary aimlessly, like a goldfish in a bowl, I would yell and direct my frustration above the sound of the engine towards the same grazing animals in adjacent fields at repeated intervals. They just looked back with indifferent expressions and occasionally summed up my anger by pissing or dumping in excessive amounts!

At times as I found myself drifting off in a trance-like

state, I would think of past acquaintances like Derek Blower, who I worked alongside whilst working for the Met Police. When I first saw Derek, he presented himself as a formidable, frightening and intimidating character. He had close-shaven hair, a full beard and jeans that were too short for him. As I sat on the old decrepit mower, I remember writing a limerick about his encounter with a piece of machinery that rhymed with his name:

A Close Shave
There was a man called Blower
Who got run down by a mower
The result of his plight
Was his hair shaved tight
And his jeans won't reach any lower

Once, when the sit-on mower broke down for the umpteenth time, I brought my own garden mower to the ground. It cut closer and generated wonderfully defined lines but took me *two whole days* to complete the task! Players remarked at how good the ground looked but had no idea how close I came to walking out the ground and going on a tour of Britain's motorways with my petrol-engine mower like Forrest Gump!

Occasionally, I would bring old friends together to play invitational, friendly games of cricket, as in the case of one match where we played 'The Rock' team at Almond-bury.

It was a sunny Sunday morning and I managed to persuade my son Harry to play as a 'ringer' to both boost our chances and fulfil my request to play alongside him once again.

As I walked into the pavilion, I noticed a nice array of freshly made sandwiches and looked forward to sampling them with a nice cup of tea... if I could get in before Harry!

The previous evening, most of the participating players had attended a wine presentation put together by me and Clive Jones to raise money for Cartworth Moor. We fervently celebrated having raised a thousand pounds, partly because I generously and selflessly waived the cost of the wine we tasted, even though Clive had paid for it!

After coming in to deliver the opening ball my first over, I turned to Dave Murdoch (Doc) a friend and fellow bowler and asked him if he too felt a little worse for wear after the previous night's imbibement.

"No, I'm fine, mate."

"Just me then?"

I slowly walked back to my mark and delivered the second ball of the over, which claimed the first wicket. A volley of cheers went up, but my own excitement was short-lived as I was overcome by a peculiar feeling. My body felt limp and I dropped the ball. Much to the bewilderment of both teams, I made my apologies and stumbled back to the clubhouse.

Dizzy, disorientated and sapped of any strength, my legs had turned to rubber bands and could barely support my weight. I staggered to and fro across my intended path back, rather like a merchant ship zig-zagging to avoid the possibility of being torpedoed but feeling like I had already been hit!

Unsurprisingly, the boys carried on playing, oblivious of my difficulties and Norman Wisdom impersonation... "Mister Grimsdale, MR GRIMSDALE!"

I summoned all my strength and barely managed to make it up the bank to the pavilion before I collapsed in a heap on the grass. Now, my plight had eventually come to the attention of the teams and they made their way across, encircling me, cracking a few jokes about being hungover, sharing the limitations of their medical knowledge and generally being of as much use as a water-mattress on a bed of nails.

Thankfully, the woman who was making the tea, immediately concluded that I was having a heart attack and rang the emergency services.

At this point, Harry, showing some distress, asked if he could help me and I erroneously whispered to him to raise my legs, instead of helping me to adopt a 'W' seated position, with my hands clasped around my legs. By this time, I was so weak and having great difficulty drawing breath, that I virtually 'shut down' to concentrate on sucking what little air I could into my lungs. I could still hear perfectly well though.

It wasn't too long before an ambulance arrived on the scene and a paramedic asked the group to stand back and take the children inside… "because the situation could turn nasty."

"I can hear, you insensitive bastard!" – I thought quietly to myself.

"What's your name?" (I didn't have the strength to reply – *although I wanted to*!)

"What's his name?" My colleagues rallied momentarily and fulfilled this part of the rescue.

"He's unconscious!"

"*No I'm not*!" I thought of the unresponsive 'Edward Longshanks' in *Braveheart* and worried about my saviour putting a thousand volts through me, in an effort to shock me back into life!

After confirming my worst fears, my practical-minded paramedic rang for the air-ambulance, stating that this method of transport would be most efficient as it could land on the pitch.

My imagination ran riot as I thought of an airlift of a wounded soldier on *M.A.S.H.*

The radio crackled and I heard the ensuing conversation as clear as day:

"We're twenty minutes away. Get yourself off to Leeds. Any hold-ups and we'll close and land on the M62."

"My God, these boys are bloody heroes!" – *I thought*!

"Wipe his body down with a towel. I can't stick down these sensors."

I was sweating profusely; a familiar characteristic of a heart-attack victim.

They quickly got me onto a stretcher and into the back of the vehicle. I don't know why, but I felt some remorse at not having sampled those sandwiches, but more oddly, I thought about the ten pairs of new shoes that were still on the top of my wardrobe, that wouldn't get to be worn by me.

For the third time in my life, I was a passenger in an ambulance with the sirens wailing, heading off to hospital.

On the twenty-minute journey to Leeds Infirmary, the paramedic continued to have great difficulty in affixing sensors to my torso. As he relentlessly struggled to find a dry patch anywhere on my body, his long beard was trailed backwards and forwards across my face. Although I wanted to, I couldn't draw enough breath to sneeze and thought this was not the way I wanted to fall off my perch...being ultimately tickled to death!

When we arrived at A and E and the doors were flung open, I was aware of a large crash team working hastily and professionally. A nurse held my hand and explained what they were going to do. Somehow, with my eyes still shut, I managed to find the strength to reply:

"These actors on *Casualty* have no idea what a real crisis is all about."

Amidst the ensuing laughter, I genuinely laid back a

felt ready to 'let go'. At that point, I didn't know whether I would come back as I slipped into unconsciousness.

There is a shortfall in words of the admiration and gratitude that I feel towards the paramedics, air-ambulance crew, surgeons and nurses, that brought me back to life. So much so, that I could never contemplate going into private care, when I value the sterling work that our National Health Service provides.

When I came round and found that I could breathe more easily, I was faced with a circle of concerned faces bearing down on me:

"Hi love, shouldn't you be somewhere else, a bike ride with the kids perhaps?"

Gwynneth doesn't normally swear! My siblings had got the message and spent the three hours travelling up from the south in a state of anxiety. A short while after this near-miss, my sister Barbara handed me a small gift that she had purchased. It was a carved heart with a pivotal lid, that I slid open to reveal a hand-written message inside. It merely said:

"You are a complete wanker!"

"You're right, Auntie Barbara," said Harry in a discerning tone.

Once again, an endearing insult had been taken to its highest accolade.

I subsequently learnt that two stents had been inserted into my left main coronary artery. It has been mooted that the traumatic injury to my sternum, had left a 'kink' in my artery, where blood had eddied and deposited cholesterol in an isolated spot.

After, initial problems such as passing out spontaneously with wrong drug dosages and the effects on blood pressure and thinning, physical recovery was relatively quick with superb aftercare. To be fair, I'm still grappling with the psychological effects of my 'event', but gosh, how my mind has been put on high alert, in terms of an acute awareness of a second chance and the beauty of life and the surrounding environment. I still swear at the television when the news comes on!

So that's it. I'm still doing voluntary work, including building projects for family and friends and counting my lucky stars. I have a wonderful family and two beautiful grandchildren and my son plays a better standard of cricket than I ever did. He must have got that talent from his grandfather, though more likely from an extraordinary amount of teaching by his coach Richard Horner.

In terms of teaching and headship, I believe I was fair and made sure those who worked hard got promoted. In truth, I've no time for poor teachers who don't improve with support and lack the right motivation to make a difference to individuals; no matter how challenging they may be. Children ultimately want to trust us and rely on the safety of our support and guidance. We bring them into this world and have a responsibility to turn them into honourable, respectful and tolerant citizens.

How would I describe my style of teaching? Unorthodox yes, con-artist and actor yes…doesn't every teacher need to be? But I was also child-centred, excellent at imparting knowledge, understanding and progressing those who wanted to learn; including parents who wanted to do well by their children. My wife and I championed the underdog and helped more able children to pursue their potential. I say pursue, because if like me, you believe in lifelong learning, then we'll never reach our full potential.

It feels like I have climbed a mountain. Fourteen Ofsteds, one heart attack later and one bet finally won.

ABOUT THE AUTHOR

Paul Franklin B.Ed (Hons) is a retired Headteacher after twenty-five years in the profession. All of his work has been drawn from life experiences, with each of his poems or songs having an anecdotal backdrop. Over the years his pupils and staff have provided the necessary approval for the subject matter of his printed work.